OREGON FESTIVALS
A GUIDE TO FUN, FRIENDS, FOOD & FRIVOLITY

JOHN SHEWEY

D0964077

WESTWINDS
PRESS®

Library of Congress Cataloging-in-Publication Data

Names: Shewey, John, author.
Title: Oregon festivals : a guide to fun, friends, food, and frivolity /
    by John Shewey.
Description: [Berkeley, California] : WestWinds Press, an imprint of
    Graphic Arts Books, [2019] | Includes index.
Identifiers: LCCN 2018024579 (print) | LCCN 2018046462 (ebook) |
    ISBN 9781513261867 (ebook) | ISBN 9781513261843 (pbk.) |
    ISBN 9781513261850 (hardcover)
Subjects: LCSH: Festivals--Oregon--Guidebooks. | Oregon--Guidebooks. |
    Oregon--Description and travel.
Classification: LCC GT4810.O7 (ebook) | LCC GT4810.O7 S54 2019 (print) |
    DDC 394.269795--dc23
LC record available at https://lccn.loc.gov/2018024579

Proudly distributed by Ingram Publisher Services.

WestWinds Press®
is an imprint of

GRAPHIC ARTS
BOOKS®

GraphicArtsBooks.com

GRAPHIC ARTS BOOKS
Publishing Director: Jennifer Newens
Marketing Manager: Angela Zbornik
Editor: Olivia Ngai
Design & Production: Rachel Lopez Metzger

CONTENTS

THE OREGON VIBE

Oregonians have a good thing going and they know it.

Oregon is a fun place to live and play; the state exudes good times and adventure, largely because of its tremendous variety. Oregon is the nation's ninth-largest state, and one of the least homogeneous in many ways—the climate, the geography, the population density, the politics, and the culture vary so much from region to region. The Portland Metro Area holds more than half of the state's entire population, and Western Oregon as a whole far surpasses the population east of the Cascade Mountains. This formidable range, with its snow-capped volcanic peaks, effectively cleaves the state in two distinct parts, not just geographically, but also in many ways culturally and demographically. Yet, while rural Oregonians might find little political and sociological common ground with the state's urban residents, both camps almost always agree on one thing: Oregon rocks!

Oregonians will celebrate just about anything, and they have plenty to celebrate. Oregon festivals come in so many forms that some are difficult to categorize, ranging from the farcical to the funny to the farfetched to the fascinating. The state's eclectic mix of festivals, from tiny small-town, off-the-radar events to massive, nationally famous gatherings, engenders a subset of Oregonians who revel in these celebrations, taking in many of them over the course of a year. I'll call them festivarians, to coin a phrase, and some of them are genre-specific, hitting as many music fests or film fests or beer fests as possible; others are generalists, embracing many kinds of festivals. Other Oregonians have their favorite events, returning year after year, while many like to check out a different event here and there. Whatever your own motivation, rest assured Oregon has a festival for you.

Those beer festivals deserve special mention. Oregon is a leader in the world of craft brewing (not to mention winemaking), and beer festivals are ubiquitous, ranging from sprawling extravaganzas featuring many dozens of breweries at big-event venues to intimate celebrations held at pubs and other small spaces and dedicated to specific kinds of beers. Beer fests also come and go—every year new beer events hit the scene; some last a few years and a few persist. In this book, I've tried to stick to those with some staying power, but the one-offs and the newcomers looking for traction are certainly worth exploring.

Oregon also hosts a variety of festivals that celebrate the natural world, and why not? The state is rich in natural history, wildlife, wild places, and people who relish them. Some festivals are dedicated to birds, others to salmon, even some to such wild edibles as mushrooms and berries. Oregon also boasts a vibrant music scene, with a variety of music festivals, big and small, all over the state. Film festivals are also big attractions, and of course Oregon's wine country, as well as the state's multifaceted agricultural business, have spawned many different festivals.

A substantial percentage of the state's annual and ongoing festivals are described herein, but not all of them. Choosing festivals to include in this book required just a few limitations. First, certain festival-type events are ubiquitous: harvest festivals, July 4 celebrations, rodeos, Octoberfests, for example, and I've opted generally not to include these (with a few notable exceptions). Second, I tried to eliminate from consideration any festival that was not ongoing—readers would not be well served to read about a festival only to discover it no longer occurs.

In an effort to make this book as complete as possible, I vigorously searched myriad sources to discover festivals big and small. The only qualifications for being included were that the festival be both annual and ongoing. A number of festivals are not included because I was not able to procure graphics from them or because they declined to provide the permission required for their graphics to be reproduced herein. In a few cases, festivals declined my invitation to be included, and with respect for the wishes of those festival organizers, those events are not included in this book. In other cases, the festival organizers simply never responded to my inquiries and requests.

But most festivals were happy for the exposure, thrilled for a chance to share their message—and their joyous celebration—with a larger audience. In total this book includes well more than 130 festivals, all over the state, at all times of year. So for the festivarians out there, for curious Oregonians and visitors—for food lovers, beer lovers, wine lovers, music lovers, and above all, fun lovers—this book is your one-stop resource.

AN OREGON FESTIVAL PRIMER

Oregon festivals come in so many forms and sizes that making generalizations about them is always difficult. Nonetheless, festival goers can enhance their experiences substantially by following some general guidelines. Each festival has its own set of rules for attendees and most all of them make things as simple and convenient as possible. When in doubt, always check with the festival itself with questions about specific policies. Many events offer FAQ pages on their websites; for those that don't, a quick phone call or short email will usually garner the answers you need.

A few basics: in most cases, pets are not allowed at festivals, but certainly not all cases. In fact, quite a few events welcome well-behaved dogs on leash, and two festivals are actually dedicated to dogs: Dog Days of Summer Oregon Coast Brew Fest (see page 150) by Rogue Ales & Spirits, and Dogtoberfest (see page 50), a collaboration between Lucky Lab Brew Pub and DoveLewis Emergency Animal Hospital. If you bring your dog, be sure to have handy poop bags, water, and a small water dish of some kind. But be mindful of the time of year—hot weather during summer can be hard on Fido, so that's a good time to leave the pup at home or with good dogsitting.

Children are welcome at many, but not all, Oregon festivals. Many events are either geared heavily toward kids or include ample kid-friendly components. Even some beer festivals allow children to attend when accompanied by a parent, and some provide activities for kids, but be sure to check ahead before you pack the kids in the car; moreover, be sure to consider whether you want to attend a beer fest or similar event with the children in tow. Obviously only attendees 21 years old and over can legally sample and drink any alcoholic beverage in Oregon in compliance with Oregon Liquor Control Commission regulations, and all attendees who wish to imbibe at beer, wine, cider, spirits, and saké fests must present legal identification upon request. Many festivals dedicated to Oregon's wealth of alcoholic options offer special ticket prices and other incentives for nondrinking designated driver attendees, which recalls an important point: be sure to arrange safe transportation any time you intend to imbibe at one of these events.

And speaking of transportation, parking can be a real drag at many festivals, especially large events. But in virtually all cases, the festival itself is your best resource for parking information—typically the organizers put substantial effort into making parking as easy and convenient as possible. Most events reserve parking lots for attendees; in urban areas, such as Downtown Portland, public transportation is a great option, allowing you to park well away from the event, then use public transport to get there and back with little fuss. Whether in a big city or a tiny town far from urban centers, be courteous about parking along neighborhood streets, and when in doubt about parking in such places, ask a festival official or even a local resident. Always be aware of parade routes and vendor rows along community streets, which are generally signed against parking leading up to the events.

Travel times vary considerably in Oregon, but always give yourself some margin for error by anticipating extra traffic, time spent parking, time spent walking, and even road construction en route (especially during summer). Otherwise, driving to a festival ranges from mundane to major adventure—a road trip to some far-flung corner of the state for a festival you've never attended is great fun. And be sure to make lodging reservations well ahead of time, whether you intend to reserve a hotel room or a campsite—they all fill up fast and early in advance of popular events, and even small-town festivals out in the hinterlands can fill the limited number of rooms and campgrounds in and near small communities.

PORTLAND AREA FESTIVALS

PORTLAND AREA FESTIVALS

More than half of Oregon's population of just over 4 million people lives in the Portland metropolitan area—nearly 2.4 million residents. So it stands to reason that Portland and its conjoined satellite communities host about half of the state's festival events. They run the gamut from the benign to the bizarre and many of them center on beer; after all, Portland ranks number one on just about everybody's top beer cities in America list. The fact that you can buy a local ale at just about any cultural affair in Portland only adds to the city's reputation as one of the West's best metropolises for food, fun, and finery.

The many different kinds of festivals held annually in and around Oregon's largest city—from superb performing arts and film festivals to renowned ethnic festivals to simple, joyous neighborhood street fairs—certainly reflects the cultural diversity of Portland and its suburbs. The city hosts some astonishingly massive humdingers. The Waterfront Blues Festival, for example, draws well over 100,000 people to listen to some 150 stage acts each year. Portland also offers unique events, such as the Northwest's only saké festival, a fruit beer festival, and a variety of other intriguing festivals.

Portland and its surrounding communities can be rather daunting for festival goers in one respect: parking can range from challenging to downright frustrating, depending on the location, and popular events, naturally, compound the problem. Many metro-area festivals recommend public transport—TriMet buses and MAX light rail. Most buses have bicycle racks, and Portland is a bike-friendly city—many festivals provide bicycle corrals. Festivals held in the suburbs tend to suffer fewer parking problems.

As might be deduced by the numerous ethnic events held in Portland, the local culinary scene includes every worldwide cuisine, as well as many eateries with a Northwest flair. Whether you're visiting the Portland area for one of its many festivals or taking in a festival while there for other reasons, take time to explore. Information for visitors is available from Travel Portland, (877) 678-5263, www.travelportland.com. Portlanders are known for their friendliness and enthusiasm—conversations with locals can easily lead to great tips on under-the-radar places to eat, imbibe, and visit.

NW COFFEE BEER INVITATIONAL

Portland
Goose Hollow Inn, 1927 SW Jefferson Street
Late January
www.facebook.com/coffee.beer.378/

Home of the "best Reuben on the planet," historic Goose Hollow Inn—a Portland landmark—is also headquarters for the NW Coffee Beer Invitational, a unique craft brew festival in which more than a dozen regional breweries are tasked with creating a freshly brewed beer with locally roasted coffee—the perfect convergence of two of Oregon's most obvious addictions.

It's the only beer festival of its kind and a must-do event for Northwesterners who love exploring the delights of the region's countless beer styles—and best of all, these coffee-inspired beers are one-of-a-kind creations, concocted just for this festival; you won't find them on the shelves of your local market. This competitive but congenial event pits some of the most creative brewing minds in the business against one another, with expert judges ultimately determining the winner, who is announced in the late afternoon. Throughout the day, attendees can taste all of the coffee beers, and even ciders. This lively beer fest, which runs from noon to 7 pm on a Saturday, occurs in the big, cozy outdoor tent at Goose Hollow Inn, with live music provided by local artists. Attendees can order food from the impressive Goose Hollow Inn menu (and yes, the Reuben really is *that* good, as are the other

NW Coffee Beer Invitational features one-of-kind ales brewed with locally roasted coffees.

handcrafted sandwiches). A modest entry fee to the Invitational includes a festival logo glass and eight tasting tickets (ticket sales at the door only).

Significantly, Goose Hollow Inn was launched in 1967 by iconic Portlander Bud Clark, best remembered for being the two-term mayor of the city, from 1985 through 1992. He was also a neighborhood activist, an early advocate of neighborhood associations, and co-founder of the *Neighbor* newspaper, which became the *Northwest Examiner*. To this day, Goose Hollow Inn is still owned and operated by the Clark family and is widely lauded as a classic, comfortable, inviting neighborhood pub.

SABERTOOTH PSYCHEDELIC STONER ROCK MICRO FEST

Portland
McMenamins Crystal Ballroom and Ringler's
    Annex, 1332 W Burnside Street
Early February
www.sabertoothpdx.com

Not surprisingly, the annual Sabertooth music festival is a McMenamins event—brought to you by the brewpub kingdom whose founders have always acted a bit outside the box, from helping to change Oregon law in the early 1980s to literally creating the craft brewery scene we enjoy so much today, to preserving nearly two dozen historic structures big and small and converting them into artistic pub masterpieces.

Sabertooth celebrates psychedelic culture in general and psychedelic rock music in particular, the genre inspired by the mind-altering states produced by psychedelic substances—notable greats in this style of rock music, which appeared in the 1960s, include iconic acts such as the Grateful Dead, Pink Floyd, Jefferson Airplane, the Doors, Velvet Underground, the Who, and even the Beatles.

Sabertooth annually assembles nearly a dozen of the hottest regional bands of the genre for a two-day rockfest at the beautiful and historic McMenamins Crystal Ballroom in Downtown Portland. At the same time, McMenamins Ringlers Pub, located on the main floor of the Crystal Ballroom, serves special beers created onsite by a collaborating team of McMenamins brewers specifically for Sabertooth—samples are free, and when you find the one you like best, you can buy a pint (there's free admission to the tasting event at Ringlers, with the brewers on hand to talk beer, rock, and more). Of note, although this event celebrates psychedelic culture, no illegal activity of any sort is permitted. Also, visibly intoxicated persons are not allowed on the premises.

Both one-day and two-day tickets to Sabertooth are reasonably priced and available in advance (recommended) via the festival website or at the door.

Tables full of swag at Sabertooth Psychedelic Rock Fest.

There are two price levels: general admission and VIP, which includes early concert entry, and close-to-stage seating in a reserved area with its own bar access. Lodging options are legion in the area, of course, but a room at McMenamins Crystal Hotel (www.mcmenamins.com/crystal-hotel), home to fifty-one guest rooms, a saltwater soaking pool, and the outstanding Zeus Café, is conveniently located two blocks away.

PORTLAND INTERNATIONAL FILM FESTIVAL

Portland
Various venues
February
www.nwfilm.org/piff

For more than four decades, the Portland International Film Festival (PIFF) has delivered a tremendous billing of films from around the world, showcasing the work of both established and up-and-coming filmmakers, and providing an amazingly diverse wintertime event across the Rose City. The festival features dozens of films representing myriad genres, shown over a two-week period in February at some half-dozen Portland movie houses, including iconic landmarks such as Bagdad Theater, Laurelhurst Theater, and Cinema 21, as well as Whitsell Auditorium, which is home to the Northwest Film Center, host of this much-anticipated festival.

Each year, PIFF selects a wide range of films—powerful dramas, thought-provoking documentaries, whimsical comedies, unique animated creations, kid-friendly movies, and much more. The festival website categorizes the films and provides a synopsis of each, making it easy to decide what movies you want to see. Included in the lineup is a late-night series of films screened at the beautiful Bagdad Theater (opened in 1927 and renovated by McMenamins in 1991); the late-night movies, special treats for adventurous devotees of late-night thrills, include genre-bending films that provocatively push boundaries. Moreover, PIFF annually highlights the works of many first-time and up-and-coming directors from around the world, providing an outstanding opportunity for attendees to enjoy films difficult to find outside of special festivals like PIFF. All told, PIFF annually screens more than 100 films. Audience members at PIFF screenings enjoy the rare privilege of voting for their favorite works to decide winners of

A full house enjoys a screening at the Portland International Film Festival.

the Audience Awards for Best Film, Best Director, Best New Director, Best Documentary, and Best Short Film.

All films are screened in their original languages with English subtitles unless otherwise noted in the PIFF program. Modestly priced general-admission and student-price tickets to individual films are available in advance (see website) as well as the day of at the theater box offices pending availability of seats—though advance purchase assures you'll have a seat, as many films sell out. The PIFF also offers ticket bundles as well as full festival passes. Most films are shown twice during the festival, but some are shown only once—all the more reason to leave nothing to chance by purchasing tickets in advance.

The film festival kicks off with an opening-night extravaganza featuring a special film screening, and co-hosted by a handful of well-known regional wineries, breweries, and food vendors. Tickets for opening night (advance purchase only via the website) sell out very quickly when they go on sale midwinter.

BREWSTILLERY FESTIVAL

Portland
Stormbreaker Brewing, 832 N Beech Street
Late February
www.stormbreakerbrewing.com/brewstillery.html

The pairing of food and beverage—the supposed art of choosing just the right drink to complement a particular edible—may well reach its zenith in the Northwest. Culinary aficionados, or "foodies," often go to extreme or perhaps excessive lengths to match just the right wine with favorite foods. And it hardly ends with wines; foodies also seek the perfect harmony between cuisine and beer, spirits, saké, and even ciders.

Such enthusiasm for pairing is part of what makes the annual Brewstillery Festival so much fun—it's partly a whimsical nod to the infatuation with pairing in the Northwest and entirely an enthusiastic celebration of the region's vibrant craft beer culture and burgeoning, increasingly creative distilled spirits infatuation. In this one-of-a-kind event, the brains behind Stormbreaker, Dan Malech and Rob Lutz, invite nearly twenty of the region's best brewers and a like number of the state's top distilleries to team up for the perfect pairing of ale and spirit. Attendees enjoy the unique opportunity to taste the results, sampling the duos in the form of a four-ounce beer pour and a quarter-ounce sampling of the associated distilled spirit.

Modestly priced tickets to the event are available by advance purchase and at the door, and include a logo beer tasting glass and ten

Brewstillery Festival features intriguing pairings of ales and spirits.

tasting tickets; VIP tickets include both a branded beer glass and branded whiskey glass, fifteen tasting tickets, and early entry to the event, which is held at Stormbreaker Brewing, a Portland favorite perhaps best known for its Mississippi Red dry-hopped red ale. The brewery's excellent food from a diverse menu is available throughout the Brewstillery Festival, which runs from noon to 8 pm. Leading up to Brewstillery, Stormbreaker runs a special mission in which the public is asked to help find the festival mascot, Tank-O; look for him at the tap and tasting rooms of the festival participants starting in January. Once you find him, take a photo and post to Instagram with #wheresTankO. Prizes are awarded for those who find the most Tank-Os.

HILLSDALE BREWFEST

Portland
Hillsdale Brewery & Public House,
   1505 SW Sunset Boulevard
Late February
www.mcmenamins.com/hillsdale-brewfest

Not only is Hillsdale Brewery & Public House among the oldest of the nearly five dozen McMenamins establishments, it also hosts the longest-running McMenamins festival. This popular Portland landmark first opened its doors in 1984 as the Hillsdale Pub, following closely on the heels of McMenamins Barley Mill and Greenway Pub. Then in 1985, thanks to tireless lobbying at the

Oregon State Capital by the McMenamin brothers, Mike and Brian, and a cadre of other now-legendary Oregon brewers, the legislature passed a landmark law that made it legal both to brew and sell beer on one property. McMenamins Hillsdale Brewery was fired up, and in October of 1985 it became Oregon's first brewpub since Prohibition and the birthplace of several of the now-classic McMenamins beers: Hammerhead, Ruby, and Terminator. To this day, Hillsdale Public House displays the original brew sheet from its first brew.

Moreover, since 1995, Hillsdale Public House has hosted the annual Hillsdale Brewfest in which McMenamins brewmeisters send their latest, greatest concoctions to compete for the coveted championship belt. Patrons determine the winner: the pub offers up trays of beer samples, arranged from lightest to darkest, and then festival goers decide who deserves the coveted title. The beers cover the spectrum of brew styles, ranging from Hefeweizen to oatmeal stout, barleywine to smoked amber ale, and beyond—the beermaking autonomy of McMenamins, wherein brewers at the various facilities are allowed and encouraged to experiment and create, is on full display in this people's-choice-style event. Each taster casts one ballot that lists his or her top three choices (and beware the shameless vote-mongering by the competing brewers, who are only too happy to mix with the throngs of attendees and lobby for votes).

The winner of the Hillsdale Brewfest enjoys the honor of assisting in the development of the beer that will represent McMenamins at the Oregon Brewers Festival later in the year. The Hillsdale Brewfest has no admission fee; the sample trays, with about ten beer samples, typically cost about $10 each. The pub has a full food menu, and the event runs from 11 am until 1 am on a Saturday.

A table full of tastings at the popular Hillsdale Brewfest held at iconic Hillsdale Brewery & Public House.

LUCKY LABRADOR
BARLEYWINE FESTIVAL

Portland
Lucky Labrador Beer Hall, 1945 NW Quimby Street
Early March
www.luckylab.com

Since 1994, Lucky Labrador Brew Pub has served as a model for the neighborhood pub concept, each of its locations providing a relaxed and convivial hangout for Portlanders who love great beer, good times, and fun food. And just a few years after opening its doors, this popular brewery launched one of the first and very few barleywine tasting events in the nation and the only one in Oregon, the annual Lucky Labrador Barleywine Festival held at the Lucky Lab Quimby Brew Hall in the Slabtown District just north of Downtown Portland.

Despite the potentially confusing moniker, barleywine is not a wine, not even in part; the wine part of the name derives from the high alcohol content of these beastly beers—typically from 8 to 12 percent, nearly that of many wines. Barleywines are big, bad, bold ales that come in two forms, with lots of middle ground; so-called American-style barleywines tend to display some hoppy bitterness in the flavor profile, while British-style barleywine beers tend to lack the bitterness, tending towards the malty end of the spectrum—traditionally at least. In the ever-creative Northwest brewing culture, such demarcations are definitely blurred, and barleywines come in an amazing array of flavor profiles, not to mention colors.

And there's no better place to explore all those barleywine incarnations than the Lucky Labrador Barleywine Festival, which annually assembles more than sixty different big bad beers, with twenty-five on tap at a time, representing a wide range of Oregon brewers, from longtime favorites to little-known nano-breweries. Luckily for beer fest junkies, this event remains a bit under the radar, even in its third decade, so crowds are modest and lines minimal.

The Lucky Labrador Barleywine Festival features high-octane specialty ales.

The easy-on-the-wallet entry fee includes a commemorative festival glass and four tasting tokens, with additional tokens available for purchase. No worries if you can't settle on a high-octane barleywine to your liking—you can always find a great Lucky Lab beer (brewed onsite), with plenty to choose from, to suit your palate, and the excellent food choices include traditional-style pizzas, zesty salads, and classic deli sandwiches. The barleywine festival runs Friday and Saturday, noon to 10 pm both days.

CIDER RITE OF SPRING

Portland
Location varies
Late March
www.nwcider.com and www.facebook.com/nwcider/

Oregon's rapidly growing cider industry has not only spawned many innovative and interesting cider varieties but also spurred the launch of a variety of festivals that celebrate these fruit-based fermented beverages that have taken the Northwest by storm.

One of the best of these cider extravaganzas is the Cider Rite of Spring, presented annually by the Northwest Cider Association and awarded "Best Northwest Cider Festival" by *Sip Northwest* magazine in 2015. Held in late March, at a time when cherry and other fruit trees are blooming in Western Oregon, Cider Rite of Spring celebrates both Northwest cider and the arrival of spring, and features some three dozen cider producers serving about 100 different cider varieties. The event is a virtual who's who of regional cider makers, with past participants including such stalwarts as 2 Towns Cider, Bull Run Cider, Finnriver Farm & Cidery, Portland Cider Company, Reverend Nat's Hard Cider, Tieton Cider Works, and many others, both big and small, from all over the Northwest.

In addition to a bedazzling array of ciders, the event offers featured food vendors and a dedicated pop-up retail store

Tasting tickets ready for action at the annual Cider Rite of Spring.

where festival attendees can buy their favorite ciders to take home. Cider Rite of Spring is a 21-and-over event, and the entry fee includes a festival logo glass and tasting tickets. VIP passes include access to catered tastings of special showcase ciders. Tickets are available in advance (see the event website or Facebook page) and at the door. The Cider Rite of Spring outgrew its original location, with capacity crowds throughout the event; see the event website for news on the current venue.

NANO BEER FEST

Portland
John's Marketplace, 3535 SW Multnomah Boulevard
April
www.nanobeerfest.com

You'll feel as if you're giddily sharing secrets among close friends. The secrets are tiny-batch ales produced by the micro-est of microbrewers, some of them on the rise ultimately to higher outputs, some of them happy to remain in the nano-brewery realm. Either way, when you attend the Nano Beer Fest, launched in 2008, you get to experience craft beers that few people ever have an opportunity to sample.

The lineup each year features nearly three dozen cutting-edge brewers, whose nano-batch offerings run the gamut of beer styles. With each annual incarnation, Nano Beer Fest welcomes a who's who of Northwest brewers you've never heard of, with recent attendees including the likes of Ridgewalker Brewing, The Hoppy Brewer, Leikum, Humble Brewing, Hop Haus, Wolf Tree Brewery, Shattered Oak, Bent Shovel Brewing, Pono Brewing, Cooper Mountain Aleworks, and many more, with the lineup changing annually. It's a tough, competitive business, and nano breweries (not to mention large breweries) come and go often in the Northwest, but for those starting up and those that survive, the annual Nano Beer Fest serves as a showcase event and includes small-batch cider and mead producers.

Nano Beer Fest spotlights some of the region's smallest ale producers.

Held outdoors at John's Marketplace, this 21-and-over-only festival runs for two days, usually a Friday and Saturday, from midday to early evening. Tickets (usually around $20) include a commemorative glass and sample tokens, with extra tokens available for purchase. Attendees have a chance to win raffle prizes throughout the day. For advance ticket purchase, public transportation details, and parking information, visit the event website.

NORTHWEST ANIMATION FESTIVAL

Portland
Hollywood Theatre, 4122 NE Sandy Boulevard
Mid-May
www.nwanimationfest.com

If your experience with animation begins and ends with the Cartoon Network, the Northwest Animation Festival will open your eyes to an amazingly artistic world of independent animation artists and their wonderful films that run the full spectrum of genres. Without million-dollar budgets, these films rarely reach a broad audience and that's why this five-day film fest extravaganza presents more than 200 animated films each year (and then continues the fun in Eugene a week later), screening both new works by acknowledged masters and art from talented amateurs.

Showcasing all forms of animation—hand drawn, computer generated, stop motion, experimental techniques, and more—Northwest Animation Festival screens films at Portland's historic Hollywood Theatre (and Eugene's iconic Bijou Cinema), with social gatherings and special events held at The Magnolia wine bar across the street. Animated films screened during the festival include many international works, and

Portland's historic Hollywood Theatre hosts the Northwest Animation Festival.

the lineup each year features every imaginable theme—comedy, action, adventure, drama, romance, and more. The festival also offers special events with animators and their work, allowing attendees an intimate look at the processes involved in making animated characters come to life.

Tickets for Northwest Animation Festival are available through the event website, with both three-day and full-festival passes available that include admission to any and all films and special events. Alternately, you can review the festival schedule and purchase tickets to the categories that interest you most. Advance purchase is wise, as the shows tend to sell out; leftover tickets are available for purchase at the box office.

Northwest Animation Festival is the brainchild of animator Sven Bonnichsen: in 2007, Portland hosted the Platform International Animation Festival, screening more than 400 films and generating substantial enthusiasm around the country. But no follow-up event occurred, spurring Bonnichsen to action. His goal with Northwest Animation Festival was to create a large local community of impassioned enthusiasts and inspired artists, and an internationally recognized hub of animation culture.

TUALATIN RIVER BIRD FESTIVAL

Sherwood
Tualatin River National Wildlife Refuge,
   19255 SW Pacific Highway
Third weekend in May
www.friendsoftualatinrefuge.org

Located on the outskirts of Portland just ten minutes west of busy Interstate 5 and 2.5 miles north of Sherwood, 1,856-acre Tualatin River National Wildlife Refuge is one of about a hundred urban national wildlife refuges in the country. Situated within the floodplain of the Tualatin River, the refuge preserves a rich diversity of habitat types—verdant riparian corridors, mixed woodlands, expansive seasonal wetlands, savannah-like grasslands, and more. The refuge attracts a wide variety of migratory and wintering water birds, as well as myriad nesting bird species, with a total count of some 200 species, not to mention more than 50 species of mammals and 25 species of reptiles and amphibians. Anchored by a large visitor center with interpretive displays, photo displays, overlooks, a huge viewing window with spotting scopes, a nature store, and more, the refuge features a network of trails with options for visitors of all abilities, along with a host of educational activities and special events.

American widgeon are among the many birds that use Tualatin National Wildlife Refuge.

One of the biggest events at the refuge is the annual one-day Tualatin River Bird Festival held each May, which offers a host of fun educational activities for all ages. The festival is organized and hosted by the Friends of Tualatin River National Wildlife Refuge, a nonprofit dedicated to supporting the mission of the refuge, in conjunction with the US Fish and Wildlife Service. Guided birding tours begin first thing in the morning at 5:30 am and thereafter, providing visitors a chance to learn to identify a variety of species by sight and sound. Tours are led by US Fish and Wildlife Service staff who work on the refuge as well as various guest birding experts.

The main festival begins at 10 am and includes a host of activities that kids can really sink their teeth into: building birdhouses (or bat or butterfly houses) to take home, archery and fishing lessons, decoy painting, gyotaku (Japanese fish painting), BB gun range, fish-migration putt-putt golf, and more. A festival favorite are the live birds of prey from Audubon Education Birds, presented by expert handlers and wildlife rehab specialists. Throughout the day, a variety of exhibitors provide educational offerings, with many local and regional conservation and resource-management groups and agencies represented. All the events and activities—including the guided bird walks— are free. Just show up and enjoy a wonderful day on one of Western Oregon's great national wildlife refuges. Activities vary from year to year and a listing of these can be found on the Friends website by April of each year.

Parking for the festival is offsite (see event website for locations). From the parking area, shuttle buses run continuously to the refuge between the hours of 5 am to 5 pm. TriMet (route 93) also stops at the refuge headquarters.

UPPER CLACKAMAS
WHITEWATER FESTIVAL

Estacada
Carter Bridge Day Use Area,
   17 miles southeast of Estacada on SR 224
Late May
www.upperclackamasfestival.org

Launched, so to speak, in 1984 by the Northwest Rafter's Association, the Upper Clackamas Whitewater Festival is a weekend of fun, exciting (and safe) whitewater activities, annually rallying hundreds of attendees and competitors who share a love of boating swift rivers in a variety of watercraft. Whitewater enthusiasts comprise a passionate and dedicated family, and this weekend-long festival has become a popular and high-spirited gathering. Even nonboaters enjoy watching the competitive events for rafts and kayaks of various kinds, as well as stand-up paddleboards.

The river races begin Saturday morning and feature a variety of classic events: oar boat slalom, paddle boat slalom, cataraft slalom, drift boat slalom, inflatable kayak mass start, hard-shell kayak mass start, inflatable kayak slalom, and the Boater X Kayak Race, in which heats of four kayakers compete for points toward the Western Whitewater Championship Series. All the races course through multistep Carter Falls, a Class IV drop that requires advanced whitewater skills, and qualified boaters can register in advance or onsite for the races (the modest race entry fees must be paid in cash onsite).

The whitewater fest also includes several unique and entertaining events. One of the most popular is the inner-tube slalom race, which draws lots of enthusiastic onlookers: racers in inner tubes challenge Carter Falls, trying to hit

Competitors run the course at the Upper Clackamas Whitewater Festival.

as many slalom gates as possible. Another crowd favorite is Val's Volleyball, in which cataraft experts must try to keep "Wilson," a giant white inflatable, between the pontoons while navigating the slalom course—and Wilson can't be touched by hand, only by boat and oars. The Cataraft Rodeo also draws enthralled crowds eager to watch some of the region's most skilled cat-boat drivers perform stunts while navigating the course, with judges awarding points for surfing holes, trick maneuvers, and showmanship.

In addition to the races, the Upper Clackamas Whitewater Festival includes a variety of free clinics and demonstrations on Saturday, and after the races, attendees and participants are invited to a picnic and beer gardens with live music until 9 pm. The festival's vendor section features the top names in whitewater gear, along with various river advocacy groups. The festival venue, Carter Bridge Day Use Site, and the swift, beautiful Clackamas River, is seventeen miles upstream (southeast) from Estacada via State Route 224.

PORTLAND ROSE FESTIVAL

Portland
Various venues
Late May to mid-June
www.rosefestival.org

Oregon's largest and most storied festival, the Portland Rose Festival occupies more than two weeks with a vast array of activities and events that annually draw more than a million attendees to celebrate eclectic Portland and spotlight the city's diverse culture. Launched in 1908, the Rose Festival began as a publicity campaign for the then-burgeoning city, and more than a century later this incredible multipronged event, which seamlessly melds contemporary flair with palpable nostalgia, was proclaimed Portland's official festival. Portland Rose Festival includes three popular parades, a massive carnival-like fair, numerous concerts featuring well-known musicians, the ever-popular Rose Festival Queen coronation, several running events, and much more.

Rose Festival kicks off on a Friday afternoon with the opening of CityFair at Tom McCall Waterfront Park, with opening-day fireworks following in the evening. Running each weekend of the festival, CityFair is a sprawling family-friendly carnival with myriad vendors, carnival rides, games, live music, and much more (including a Portland Rose Festival museum exhibit). The music lineup is announced on the Rose Festival website and over the years has included an intriguing mix of artists and music genres. Opening weekend also brings the whimsical Rose Festival Point One Run, in which runners (and walkers, strollers, amblers, and anyone else) race a grand total of 528 feet, all within the bounds of CityFair; creative apparel is encouraged, and participants must register in advance, as is the case with all festival races. The serious running begins the next day, Sunday, with the Rose Festival Half Marathon. The festival offers two additional foot-power events: the Starlight Run—Oregon's largest fun run—features some 5,000 costumed competitors racing not only to break the tape at the finish line but also to garner prizes for best individual and group getups (and the costumes tend to be highly decorative and immensely creative). The Starlight Run follows the 3.1-mile Starlight Parade route and the entire course is lined with cheering spectators—250,000 of them. Even more spectators line the streets for the 4-mile Grand Floral Walk preceding the Grand Floral Parade. Throughout all the festival footraces, participants are treated like champs by event staff and onlookers alike.

The aforementioned parades, three of them in total, are integral to the Portland Rose Festival. The first, and one of the most popular festival events,

The Starlight Parade is one of many events included in the Portland Rose Festival.

is the Starlight Parade, which offers funky, eclectic fun for everyone. From traditional marching bands and flood-lit floats to glow-in-the-dark umbrellas and unique hand-built entries, you'll see the best of Portland's diverse community groups (and surrounding Northwest region) together in one whimsical pageant. The Starlight Parade continues a longtime festival tradition from the early 1900s, when illuminated floats built on electric trolley cars made their way through the city on trolley tracks. Today, participants light up the night with approximately 100 illuminated entries along a 2.25-mile route. The parade draws more than 325,000 spectators to Downtown Portland.

A week later comes the much-anticipated Grand Floral Parade—a beloved highlight of the festival for more than 100 years. As its name suggests, the Grand Floral Parade is regaled in floristry, or what the Japanese call ikebana, the artistic arrangement of flowers. This parade courses for four miles, draws hundreds of thousands of spectators, and features a bedazzling lineup of colorful floats, most all of them bedecked in vibrant flowers that so define the Rose City. Prior to the parade, the Rose Festival Queen coronation is held in the Veterans Memorial Coliseum, culminating three months of activities for the high school women who comprise the Rose Festival Court.

Scheduled to fall between the two extravagant parades, the annual Junior Parade is also a longtime Rose Festival tradition in which kids, dressing in costume, transform wagons into floats, decorate their bikes with colorful flowers, or just parade with their pets (and parents). Elementary and middle school marching bands fill the Hollywood District with song, and dance teams add swirls of color to the celebration.

The Portland Rose Festival also features a variety of waterfront activities, including hosting the annual Dragon Boat Races, a Chinese cultural tradition in which paddle teams race beautifully crafted wooden boats festooned with colorful dragon head designs. Portland's races annually draw nearly 100 teams from around the country and beyond. Far more whimsical is the family-friendly Milk Carton Boat Race, a Rose Festival standard since 1973, in which boaters compete for prizes in numerous categories in homemade hand-powered craft that float only by means of recycled milk cartoons and jugs. The ultimate prize is the coveted Best in Show milk can trophy. The Rose Festival also includes Fleet Week, during which vessels from the US Navy, US Coast Guard, and Royal Canadian Navy moor at the waterfront and invite civilians on board for scheduled ship tours. Fleet Week provides a platform for the public to thank veterans and active-duty personnel while learning about the various watercraft employed by the armed services.

Throughout its three-week run, the Portland Rose Festival offers many other activities and events, and the entire extravaganza comes to life thanks to a small, dedicated professional staff and legions of volunteers. The festival schedule, with complete details about all the events and copious useful details for attendees, is available on the festival website. Few citywide festivals in the nation can boast of such longstanding tradition and residents of the city are justifiably proud of the exciting, colorful, congenial Portland Rose Festival.

PORTLAND HORROR FILM FESTIVAL

Portland
Hollywood Theatre, 4122 NE Sandy Boulevard
Early June
www.portlandhorrorfilmfestival.com

Did you grow up mesmerized by Bela Lugosi, Lon Chaney, Boris Karloff, and the ubiquitous Vincent Price? Did you revel in the blockbuster horror films of the '70s and '80s—*The Omen, The Exorcist, Halloween*? Do you remember the cult classics of the '80s, such as *The Evil Dead, Lifeforce,* and *Night of the Comet*? Do the horror spoofs—*Scream, Scary Movie, Shaun of the Dead*—tickle your funny bone? Or maybe your nightmares are spawned by the millennial masterpieces, movies such as *The Ring, Paranormal Activity,* and *30 Days of Night.*

No matter how you like your spooky movies, the Portland Horror Film Festival will enthrall you with an outstanding lineup of under-the-radar independent works representing every subgenre of scary films—funny, gory, nerve-wracking, and flat-out scary, and all cooler and more innovative than anything you can see at the multiplex. Independent filmmakers are the ones creating fresh looks at horror, and you can see the best films from the horror masters of tomorrow at the Portland Horror Film Festival. From satanic guitars to zombie children to sweet, sweet revenge, this enthralling film fest has something for everyone, including films from the United States, Canada, Great Britain, Brazil, Sweden, Spain, Italy, the Philippines, Greece, Norway,

France, Australia, Turkey, Iran, and more.

Beginning Thursday evening and running through Saturday, the event screens all movies at the historic Hollywood Theatre, packing some four dozen films into a three-day fright fest. Each year, the festival selects several full-length features and numerous short films that range from a minute or so to about half an hour in length,

Portland Horror Film Festival features myriad films along with Q&A sessions with filmmakers.

providing chills and thrills in masterfully concise movies. In addition to the movies themselves, the Portland Horror Film Festival includes casual meet-and-greet events and post-movie Q&A sessions with visiting filmmakers, along with a Saturday evening wrap-up party and awards ceremony.

Modestly priced festival tickets deliver a lot more bang for the buck than regular movie tickets, and attendees can choose between single-day tickets or three-day full-festival tickets. Full-event tickets provide access to all films and events throughout the weekend, and all tickets are available for early purchase at the event website.

RYE BEER FEST

Happy Valley (southeast of Portland)
Happy Valley Station, 13551 SE 145th Avenue
Mid-June
www.beerheard.com/rye-beer-fest

What exactly is a rye beer? Well, as the name might suggest, it's a beer in which some portion of the barley malt is replaced with rye (usually malted rye), a lesser-known but similar grain. But there's a lot more to it than that, especially in the beercentric Northwest, and that's what Rye Beer Fest founder Kerry Finsand aims to teach ale aficionados at this flavorful and educational beer event held each year as part of the citywide Portland Beer Week.

Rye Beer Fest brings the region's best rye beers—upwards of two dozen of them—under one roof, and perhaps the first thing attendees learn is just how much wonderful variation occurs in the flavor profiles of rye beers coming from brewers throughout the state. Rye beers can be earthy, tart, or spicy, and this family-friendly event (21-and-over for

Rye beer aficionados sample the offerings at the Rye Beer Fest.

beer sampling/drinking) features a curated tap list consisting of a variety of beer styles utilizing this impactful grain. Expect rye beers ranging from saisons and IPAs to the traditional German style of Roggenbier. Each year, Rye Beer Fest features a wide assortment of breweries, from longstanding favorites to newly launched up-and-comers. Past lineups have included the likes of Stormbreaker (Portland), Ordnance (Boardman), Vagabond (Salem), Sedition (The Dalles), Bent Shovel (Oregon City), and many more.

Entry to the festival is free, but an inexpensive ticket package is needed to drink beer and includes four drink tickets (eight tickets with advance purchase online) plus the official event tasting glass; additional tickets are available for purchase (most beers cost one ticket per four-ounce sample and four tickets for a glassful). Food is available in eclectic abundance thanks to the eighteen food carts at Happy Valley Station, a you-gotta-see-it-to-believe-it innovative, 3,800-square-foot, temperature-controlled food-cart pod.

Oregon's only rye beer festival—and one of the few anywhere in the world—not only provides a joyous educational celebration of these unique ales, but also serves the community by donating proceeds to New Avenues For Youth, a local nonprofit that supports homeless and at-risk youth in Portland.

CIDER SUMMIT PDX

Portland
The Fields Neighborhood Park,
   1099 NW Overton Street
Mid-June
www.cidersummitnw.com

Portland's eclectic Pearl District hosts the region's largest cider festival each June as Cider Summit PDX gathers a truly massive assemblage of local, regional, and international ciders and cider cocktails, with some 150 choices available from dozens of producers—truly a who's who of cideries. Oregon's ever-growing cider industry is well represented at this casual and friendly Friday/Saturday event, with the state's best-known cider brands pouring samples alongside the small-batch producers. Each year, the lineup is announced on the event website, and one of the most alluring aspects of Cider Summit is its mercurial growth: each new year brings dozens of new ciders from established producers and new players alike—it's one-stop shopping for ciderites who love the ever-expanding range of ciders produced in the Northwest and beyond.

Cider Summit PDX, its many tents forming a giant circle at The Fields Neighborhood Park (consult the event website in case the venue changes), also features a variety of local food vendors, along with live music provided by well-known regional artists. In fact, the Cascade Blues Association, which helps to produce the event music lineup, is one the beneficiaries of Cider Summit PDX. Another of the beneficiaries is DoveLewis Emergency Pet Hospital, and Cider Summit PDX is dog friendly, featuring a special Dog Lounge (as usual in dog-friendly Portland, bring baggies, a leash, and only friendly furred friends). Also, during the festivities, numerous cideries compete in the Fruit Cider Challenge, the winner being crowned by vote of attendees.

Tickets are available online and at a variety of bottle shops and other retail shops in Portland (see the list on the event website). Cider Summit PDX

Cider Summit is an outdoor festival held during June in Portland's Pearl District.

(a 21-and-over-only event) offers both general admission and VIP tickets, both at modest prices. General admission tickets (available online and at the gate) include a commemorative tasting glass and a set of tasting tickets; VIP tickets (available online only) include extra tasting tickets and special early entry on Friday. Attendees can buy additional tickets onsite (bring cash). Cider Summit PDX is just one incarnation of Cider Summit, the brainchild of Alan Shapiro, founder of SBS Imports: if you miss the Portland event or just can't get enough, Cider Summit Seattle occurs in September and Cider Summit San Francisco occurs in April.

FESTIVAL OF BALLOONS

Tigard
Cook Park, 17005 SW 92nd Avenue
Late June
www.tigardballoon.org

For a weekend each June, a blue summer sky brims with colorful hot-air balloons in morning's limpid air, painting a serene and indelible panorama over Oregon's verdant Willamette Valley—this is the Festival of Balloons in Tigard. Balloon pilots from throughout the region converge on expansive Cook Park, on the banks of the Tualatin River, to put on a kaleidoscopic aerial show that can be seen for miles. But the up-close view is by far the best, and attendees soon discover that the Festival of Balloons offers much more than the flame-powered aircraft.

The balloons launch early in the morning while the air is calm—from 5:45 to 6:15—Friday, Saturday, and Sunday. Get to the park early to witness this colorful spectacle and mingle over coffee with balloon aficionados and fellow attendees. The festival doesn't offer balloon rides, but you can connect with pilots who offer such commercial services, and even sign up for an early-morning tethered ride on a first-come, first-served basis. As balloons dot the skies over Tigard, the festival's many other activities kick off, including an extensive vendor section featuring local and regional artisans and craftspeople along with commercial exhibitors, as well as the Funtastic carnival fun center brimming with entertainment for all ages. The festival main stage offers entertainment for kids during the afternoons and live music in the evenings. Food vendors offer numerous choices, and

the walk-around beer gardens allow adults to buy a pint or two and peruse the vendors rows while imbibing. On Friday and Saturday evenings, perhaps the festival's single most popular event unfolds: a variety of balloon pilots return to the field to fire up the burners on their tethered balloons in the annual Night Glow, sublimely illuminating the festival grounds to the delight of the crowds.

Fanciful balloons take to the air during the Festival of Balloons in Tigard.

The Festival of Balloons also features a six-on-six soccer tournament, eating contests, the annual Festival of Cars classic auto show, and the Twilight 5K run/walk and Twilight Run; the mile course is especially popular with kids—it's an untimed event and T-shirts for the event are available in child sizes only. The three-day admission pass to the Festival of Balloons is less than $10, and other than registration fees to enter the Twilight Run, soccer tournament, or car show competition, only the carnival rides cost extra. Bring cash for food and drinks; many of the vendors are set up for credit card transactions as well. Festival parking is available on the Tigard High School field for $5, which benefits Tigard High School (THS) Breakfast Rotary & THS Boosters. The parking entrance is at the THS Swim Center Parking Lot. There is a short walk down the Cook Park hill to the festival grounds, or you may ride the shuttle for only $1 (benefits American Cancer Society/ Relay for Life). The Festival of Balloons is produced by a nonprofit organization and raises funds for many nonprofit groups in Tigard.

SHERWOOD WINE FESTIVAL

Sherwood
Old Town Sherwood
Late June
www.sherwoodwinefestival.com

In the heart of the Willamette Valley, which was one of the earliest settled areas in the Northwest at the onset of America's westward expansion in the nineteenth century, Sherwood boasts a rich and, at times, trying history—two fires, 1896 and 1911, severely damaged the then-burgeoning little community. At the time, Sherwood had recently seen its largest employer, a brickyard built and owned by four Portland businessmen, suddenly

Medal winners at the intimate Sherwood Wine Festival.

cease production after it had brought more than 100 jobs to the small town, and many supporting enterprises. At the time the brickyard opened in 1890, the little town out in the wooded countryside was called Smockville, named for and by entrepreneur and town founder, JC Smock, who, in 1885, laid out the first nine square blocks of what would become Sherwood.

To this day, these blocks comprise Sherwood's downtown district, which in the past fifteen years has undergone significant and rejuvenating revitalization. Happily situated at the doorstep to the Willamette Valley's famous wine country, Historic Old Town Sherwood now boasts a variety of intriguing places to eat and imbibe, including 503 Uncorked, the local wine bar that hosts and sponsors the Sherwood Wine Festival held each summer.

This outdoor Saturday festival brings together a fine collection of local wineries, from longstanding favorites to little-known boutique wineries whose vintages are difficult to procure owing to limited production. Alongside excellent wines to please any palate, the festival also hosts several breweries and a variety of local food vendors, all in a relaxing atmosphere, and usually under a bright sunny sky, and always to the accompaniment of live music throughout the day. Modestly priced tickets (purchase on the event website or onsite) include a commemorative tasting glass. Launched in 2016, the Sherwood Wine Festival remains intimate, an appealing alternative to the numerous massively busy wine events around the region.

SAKÉ FEST PDX

Portland
Oregon Convention Center,
   777 NE Martin Luther King, Jr Boulevard
Late June
www.SakeFestPDX.com

The only event of its kind in the Northwest, Saké Fest PDX celebrates the world of saké in all its diversity and finery. Saké, sometimes inaccurately called "rice wine," is a unique beverage created through a fermentation process in which rice starch is converted to sugar, which is then converted to alcohol by yeast. Saké, which has its roots in China more than 4,000 years ago, was ultimately perfected by the Japanese beginning more than 2,000 years ago. As early as the Japanese began refining their saké-brewing techniques, the beverage served as a drink of family and friendship and celebration; saké has been an integral part of Japanese society for centuries, and its popularity continues to increase worldwide. Today, some 1,800 brewers produce about 14,000 different sakés worldwide, mostly in Japan.

Saké Fest PDX gathers together some of the finest imported saké, along with saké brands brewed right here in the United States, including Oregon. The annual lineup of brands includes all the traditional styles: Junmai, Junmai Ginjo, Junmai Daiginjo, Honjozo, Nama, Genshu, and Nigori. But this extravagant and joyous celebration hardly ends there. Along with

every traditional style and grade of saké from numerous producers, guests can try infused saké, umeshu (a liqueur made from ume fruits), saké cocktails, and more. And in addition to an amazing array of fine saké, including many premium and rare brews, Saké Fest PDX serves up a wide array of culinary delights, allowing attendees to learn why saké is far more than a beverage consumed with sushi. In fact, like wine, different saké styles and flavor profiles pair exceptionally well with a broad range of foods and this intriguing festival provides ample opportunity to match flavors and textures.

Saké Fest PDX is one of the few festivals in the world dedicated to this popular beverage.

Saké Fest PDX, launched in 2010, is a one-day ticketed affair held during the evening hours at the Oregon Convention Center ballroom (venue is subject to change, with all annual details as well as advance ticket sales on the event website). Each year a limited number of early-admission tickets is made available; they allow attendees to enjoy easy unfettered access to the food and beverage tasting tables an hour earlier than regular-admission ticket holders. Ticket prices include all samples of both food and saké at all sampling stations as well as a souvenir tasting glass. A limited number of tickets is available at the door, but advance purchase via the website is a good idea (adults 21 and older only—proper ID required for admission).

ORGANIC BEER FEST

Portland
Overlook Park, 1599 N Fremont Street
Last full weekend in June
www.organicbeerfest.org

Northwesterners love their local beers and certainly harbor a deep appreciation for sustainability, including organic food and beverage production, and both concepts converge at the Organic Beer Fest, an annual four-day celebration designed to raise awareness about organic beer and sustainable living. In recent incarnations, this popular and intriguing event has offered nearly sixty organic beers, ciders, and mead, including many brews from small-batch producers whose limited distribution assures that sampling their beverages is a rare treat.

Held in beautiful Overlook Park, this outdoor event also includes live music, food vendors, sustainability-oriented vendors, and nonprofit groups. Earth friendly, the festival includes onsite compost and recycling containers; volunteers working the event wear organic cotton and hemp T-shirts, and all event signage is reusable. Organic Beer Fest also happens to be probably the most family-friendly brew festival in the state (minors are allowed with their parents, although only attendees 21 and over can sample and drink beer, of course), and delivers one of the most amicable, relaxed atmospheres of any beer event.

Drinking requires purchase of the current year's commemorative festival cup for a nominal fee and then drink tokens for $1 each (cash only). The festival begins on Thursday afternoon, runs most of the day and into the night on Friday and Saturday, and continues from noon to 5 pm on Sunday. Organic Beer Fest offers a bike corral for cyclists, and public transportation (TriMet) is easy and convenient. However, the festival has no designated parking area and Overlook Park has only minimal parking,

Held in beautiful Overlook Park, Organic Beer Fest assembles a great lineup up Northwest organically produced ales.

making TriMet, with a major station directly in front of the park the best option for many attendees (see the event website for details); limited curbside parking is available in the adjacent neighborhood, but attendees are warned not to park in the Kaiser Permanente lots.

PORTLAND CRAFT BEER FESTIVAL

Portland
The Fields Neighborhood Park,
    1099 NW Overton Street
First weekend in July
www.portlandcraftbeerfestival.com

Portland, as well as Oregon in general, not to mention the entire Northwest, and for that matter all of the West, is neck deep in craft beer festivals—and why not? Nothing beats a great brew fest for camaraderie, conviviality, and of course craft beers. The Portland Craft Beer Festival (PCFB) celebrates all three—it's a relaxed, inviting event featuring an intriguing lineup of amazing ales representing myriad styles. But unique among the many beer festivals, PCFB features only beers (plus a few ciders and wines) brewed within the city limits of Portland.

Portland is closing in on 100 craft breweries (plus a handful of cideries, mead makers, and wineries), and in recent years they've been incredibly well represented at PCBF, with about fifty of them participating. Portland—voted America's best beer town by various media on several occasions—loves its craft beer and has more breweries than any city in the nation; the city's hopheads and malt maniacs quickly embraced PCBF, and it now draws capacity crowds.

The fest runs for three days, beginning at noon Friday, Saturday, and Sunday, and running until 10 pm on Friday and Saturday, and 7 pm on Sunday. Sunday is family day, when children can attend with their parents and enjoy a variety of outdoor lawn games. Because PCBF has become so justifiably popular, it's wise to buy advance tickets (see the event website). The festival tasting cup with ten

The three-day Portland Craft Beer Festival is one of the city's most popular beer events.

beer tickets costs about $25 (one ticket per four-ounce sample, four tickets per full pour), and additional tickets are $1 each. With an event wristband, attendees can return any day. The PCBF also offers a VIP package, which costs a bit more, and includes a special mug plus fifteen tickets that earn six-ounce samples. Availability is limited and VIP tickets may not be available at the door, so get them in advance online. The venue—The Fields Neighborhood Park—is located on the north side of the Pearl District. Street-side parking fills quickly and the nearest public pay-lots are several blocks away, so get there early or consider public transport (TriMet or MAX light rail).

WATERFRONT BLUES FESTIVAL

Portland
Tom McCall Waterfront Park by Hawthorne Bridge
Early July
www.waterfrontbluesfest.com

Portland's Safeway Waterfront Blues Festival, presented by First Tech Credit Union, is a massive musical extravaganza spanning five days and culminating in a July 4 fireworks display over the Willamette River. Since its quiet kickoff in 1988, this incredibly popular festival owned and operated by the Oregon Food Bank has raised more than $10 million and collected more than 1,000 tons of food—all to help alleviate hunger and its root causes in Oregon and Clark County, Washington.

This award-winning festival annually hosts more than 100 music acts, ranging from the biggest names in Blues to up-and-coming local singers and bands. This is largely a shoulder-to-shoulder event, particularly when well-known musicians take the stage. Each year's lineup is announced months in advance on the event website. The festival offers a variety of multiday passes, each with a different set of benefits. Five-day passes start at about $40 (with early bird pricing), making the Waterfront Blues Festival the best entertainment value for the July 4 weekend.

The festival offers myriad food and beverage vendors. Festival attendees should consider bringing a fold-up chair, and should check out the "What to Bring" section of the event website before venturing to Waterfront Park. Parking is always a challenge for an event of this magnitude, with curbside parking nearby nearly impossible; however, about a dozen pay-to-park lots (SmartPark and City Center Parking) are located within a reasonable distance. Naturally, many festival veterans have learned to get downtown early in the day and relax over a cup of coffee and perhaps breakfast somewhere in the area after finding parking as close as possible to Tom McCall Waterfront Park, the site of the event. Attendees also park across the river, on the east bank, and walk across the Hawthorne Bridge. Public transportation—MAX light rail and TriMet—is another excellent option, and TriMet runs extra buses to accommodate the event.

Waterfront Blues Festival annually features more than 100 music acts playing to huge crowds at Waterfront Park.

Bicycle riders can safely leave their bikes at either of two designated and volunteer-staffed parking locations.

Whether you're a hardcore Blues fans or a casual listener, the Waterfront Blues Festival is an event not to miss. Many attendees plan entire vacations around this colossal celebration, and each year people come from every state in the union and dozens of foreign locales, traveling from afar just for this extraordinary party. For visitors planning to spend most of the week in the Portland area for this event, consult Travel Portland, (877) 678-5263, www.travelportland.com, for information about lodging and the countless sights and activities you can enjoy in and near Oregon's largest city.

ROADHOUSE BREWFEST

Hillsboro
McMenamins Cornelius Pass Roadhouse,
    4045 NE Cornelius Pass Road
Mid-July
www.mcmenamins.com/roadhouse-brewfest

The annual Roadhouse Brewfest is a good old-fashioned outdoors summer shindig featuring around twenty different beers from McMenamins as well as other area breweries, along with a handful of craft ciders, live music from noon into the night, tours of the brewery and distillery, and guided history tours of the property, all under the beautiful July sun in this out-of-the-way, incredibly well-renovated historic property west of Portland.

Meet, mingle, and chat with brewers, enjoy food from Imbrie Hall's summertime menu, and let the kids run around all crazy-like. A not-to-be-missed summertime tradition for many Pacific Northwest beer lovers, this free-admission, laid-back party boasts a few beers crafted specifically for the event.

Cornelius Pass Roadhouse, acquired by McMenamins in 1986, is an amazing property with a lengthy history: in 1843, Kentuckian Edward Henry Lenox (1827–1905), having arrived via the Oregon Trail, staked a claim to the

McMenamins Cornelius Pass Roadhouse hosts the laid-back Roadhouse Brewfest.

property (years later, his memories of the journey were published as a small book titled *Overland to Oregon*). Around 1850, Robert Imbrie (1831–1897), who had reached Oregon a few years earlier via ship sailing around Cape Horn, acquired the Lenox farm. He built the three-story, Italian Villa-style home that still stands today.

GRESHAM ARTS FESTIVAL

Gresham
Historic Downtown District
Mid-July
www.greshamoregon.gov/ArtsFestival

Heading through Gresham on busy Division Street or Powell Boulevard, it's easy to miss the city's beautifully refurbished historic downtown district that is sandwiched between the two main arteries leading to and from nearby Portland to the west. But Gresham's eclectic downtown area offers myriad excellent options for dining, shopping, and imbibing, and also hosts a variety of special events throughout the year, including the longstanding Gresham Arts Festival, an engaging celebration featuring events for all ages.

The festival kicks off on Friday evening at 5 pm with the Art Under the Stars, where attendees can join festival artists and stroll the downtown area into the night, checking out the shops, enjoying a glass of wine, and perusing the silent auction that benefits Gresham Outdoor Public Art, all to the accompaniment of live music. Then on Saturday morning at 9, the festival proper begins, with more than 150 juried artisans

Gresham Arts Festival holds the Guinness record for the largest display of chalk pavement art.

filling the downtown streets with an array of unique handcrafted art; live cultural and musical performances continue throughout the weekend, and Gresham's shops and restaurants throw down the welcome mats.

The Kids' Village at the centrally located Gresham Arts Plaza offers all sorts of free fun activities for children, including face painting, music, and the Children's Fountain, and kids can join adults in creating the epic Chalk of Fame pavement chalk murals—a feat that set a Guinness World Record in 2015 for the largest display of chalk pavement art, subsequently beaten by a Canadian event, and then reclaimed by Gresham Arts Festival in 2017; be sure to sign up in advance on the festival website to participate in this free artistic endeavor, which goes on all day, from 9 am to 5 pm.

The Gresham Arts Festival culminates in the popular Gresham's Got Talent event held Saturday evening from 6:30 to 9:30 to showcase the wide array of talented entertainers in the community. Featuring celebrity judges, along with local food and drink, this lively event draws throngs of festive onlookers, and provides the perfect nightcap to a wonderful community arts celebration.

PORTLAND SLAVIC FESTIVAL

Portland
Ventura Park, 460 SE 113th Avenue
Midsummer
www.slavicfestivalportland.org

Have you ever tried kishka or borscht? Pierogi or pljeskavica or plov? How about bryndzové halušky? If not, it's time to attend the Portland Slavic Festival, where you can explore the world of traditional Slavic cuisine, not to mention Slavic art and culture in beautiful Ventura Park. In addition to delectable Slavic foods available from myriad vendors, this joyous celebration features nonstop live music and performing arts, as well as a variety of workshops and seminars, all designed to highlight Slavic culture and its significant contributions to Portland's harmonious coalescence of myriad ethnic groups. As such, the Portland Slavic Festival aims to attract people from all walks of life, whether to learn about Slavic history and lifestyle or to celebrate their own Slavic heritage.

Slavs comprise continental cultures tied together by a common linguistic family and ethnicity, and traditionally hail from Eastern and Southeastern

Europe. Slavs are subdivided into Western Slavs in Poland, Czechoslovakia, Slovakia, and Lusatia; Eastern Slavs, primarily in Russia, Belarusian, and the Ukraine; and South Slavs, from Serbia, Bosnia, Slovenia, Croatia, Macedonia, and Montenegro. As early as the 1860s, Slavic immigrants, primarily Russians at that time, had found their way to Oregon and the Northwest, but the

Portland Slavic Festival is popular for its food, cultural events, and sporting competitions.

largest waves of immigrants arrived starting in the 1970s after the Soviet government relaxed emigration laws for some religious groups. Today the East European Coalition estimates that some 150,000 immigrants from former Soviet countries now live in the greater Portland area, and Russian is now the third most-spoken language in Oregon, behind English and Spanish.

At this free-admission summertime festival dedicated to community and harmony, attendees can not only relish in traditional foods from Russia, Serbia, Armenia, the Ukraine, and more, but also revel in kaleidoscopic dance routines and other stage shows. The Portland Slavic Festival also features a popular soccer tournament with various divisions; consult the event website for specifics.

OREGON BREWERS FESTIVAL

Portland
Tom McCall Waterfront Park,
   300 SW Naito Parkway
Last full weekend in July
www.oregonbrewfest.com

It seems almost incredible that a pioneering micro-brew festival could successfully launch in Portland in 1988—a time when Oregon was home to a mere seven craft breweries and the entire nation had only 128 craft breweries.

All of them were invited to that very first Oregon Brewers Festival, billed as "the first gathering of and exhibit of independent brewers in the United States."

Twenty-six breweries from six states showed up, and the event drew far more attendees than its organizers anticipated. Now, more than three decades later, this five-day extravaganza draws a crowd that may soon surpass 100,000 people and attracts dozens of breweries—more than ninety in recent years. It reigns as one of the biggest and best brew fests in the country. In addition to every imaginable style of beer available by sample and by the glassful, the festival includes half a dozen outstanding food vendors, ongoing excellent live music, beer-related vendors, beer memorabilia displays, home-brewing information and demonstrations, a beer writers tent, and the Crater Lake Soda Garden with complimentary handcrafted soda for minors and designated drivers (minors must be accompanied by a parent).

Sampling and drinking beer requires the one-time purchase of a souvenir mug for a very reasonable price (there is no admission charge at the gates). Wooden beer tokens, $1 each, are required for samples; past festivals pricing has been one token for a taste and five tokens for a full mug of beer. Both mugs and tokens are available at a dedicated booth near the main entrance at SW Oak Street and Naito Parkway (cash only/ATMs on sight). During big events like this in Downtown Portland, parking can be brutal. The nearest Smart Park lot is located at SW Naito and NW Davis Street, and other public pay-lots are not too far away. Public transportation saves the headache of finding parking and then walking (or hiking, depending on how far away you end up parking), and the MAX line drops off only one block from the festival at SW First and Oak Street. The festival also has a staffed onsite bike corral where you can park your bike for free.

For craft-beer aficionados, this grandiose event can easily consume an entire day or even two or three days, so plan accordingly—in fact, given the massive list of available beers, you'd be doing yourself a disservice not to dedicate at least a full day to sampling from the amazing selection.

Oregon Brewers Festival, which celebrated 30 years in 2018, draws huge crowds to Waterfront Park and features dozens of regional breweries.

TUALATIN CRAWFISH FESTIVAL

Tualatin
Tualatin Community Park,
    8515 SW Tualatin Road
Early August
www.tualatincrawfishfestival.com

Presented By Columbia Bank

Can't make it to the huge crawfish festival in New Orleans? Worry not; the annual Tualatin Crawfish Festival is a big deal, too, founded in 1951 and annually drawing more than 15,000 people who relish not only the amazing food—consuming about 1.5 tons of crawfish each year—and all-around gaiety, but also in the myriad activities that range from competitive to whimsical. This must-see extravaganza features crawfish served in a variety of ways, along with plenty of other food choices, and adults 21 and over can wash down the cooked crustaceans with a craft beer from any of the regional breweries participating in the beer garden.

Of course no crawfish celebration would be complete without a crawfish-eating contest, and at the Tualatin Crawfish Festival it's a fan-favorite event in which contestants have a mere fifteen minutes to cram as many crawfish down their gullets as possible, eating both tail and claw meat. It's one thing to win the event but quite another to challenge the record of eating 170 crawfish, a mark that has stood since 1972 (preregistration is required for the eating contest, with details on the festival website).

The Tualatin Crawfish Festival is entirely family friendly and features a dedicated CRAWkids Zone offering numerous engaging activities, such as a dunk tank, rock wall, building area, and more. The festival also features balloon art, face painting, a water balloon toss, magician performances,

Crawfish—aka crawdads and crayfish—are, of course, the star attraction at the Tualatin Crawfish Festival.

sack races, carnival games, and a cornhole tournament. Even well-behaved dogs get in on the action—creatively costumed canines (in theme, of course) are welcome at the festival. Early Saturday morning, the starting guns sound for the Kids' Run, Crawfish Crawl Relay, and Crawfish Crawl 5K and Half Marathon (race participants receive an event shirt, a medal, sponsor-provided prizes, and even a beer at the finish line for adults). In the relay, teams of four can choose to run or walk, with each team member running three legs or walking two legs of the 2.04-mile course on forested park trails.

Tualatin Crawfish Festival also features a vendor's village with an eclectic mix of products and activities producing a spirited and interesting Saturday Market–style experience. The festival opens late Friday afternoon, with live music beginning midevening and continuing through Saturday. Annually the event hosts a variety of well-known musicians, with past entertainers including such luminaries as Curtis Salgado, Lisa Mann, and Norman Sylvester. Annually the specific mix of activities at Crawfish Fest varies, but this lively celebration always offers all-ages fun and entertainment aplenty. The deservedly popular festival culminates with a terrific fireworks show on Saturday evening. The festival draws lots of people, so parking options include the old Haggen's store lot at 8515 SW Tualatin-Sherwood Road, or you could park at Cook Park and walk through the park to get to the festival.

SPIRITSFEST

Portland
Portland Saturday Market, Waterfront Park,
   2 SW Naito Parkway
August
www.portlandsaturdaymarket.com/events

Have a drink, catch a show, shop local.

Okay, sign me up—especially for the "have a drink" part of that trifecta because in this case, the drinks come from local craft distillers. Spiritsfest, held at the Rose City's iconic Portland Saturday Market, highlights innovative Portland-area distillers who are making a mark not only in Oregon but throughout the Northwest and beyond. At this popular yet surprisingly intimate summer festival, attendees get to meet the makers of some of the region's best distillers and not only discover what they are making and bottling but also learn how to use these craft spirits to create mouthwatering cocktails of all kinds.

Each year the mix of participating distillers changes a bit, but they all arrive ready to serve up their signature cocktails and samples of their distilled spirits, including small-batch whiskies, rums, vodkas, gins, and more. The distillers sell

Spiritsfest at Portland Saturday Market celebrates the Rose City's vibrant craft distilling scene.

signature cocktails, and their spirits by the bottle, at the event. Past incarnations of Spiritsfest have hosted such stalwarts in the Portland scene as Bull Run Distilling, Indio Spirits, Miru Vodka, Thomas and Sons Distilling, Vivacity Spirits, Big Bottom Whiskey, Eastside Distilling, and Wild Roots Spirits. The event is 21 and over, and admission is free.

Operating since 1974, Portland Saturday Market is the largest continually operating outdoor arts and crafts market in the nation. Located in Portland's historic Old Town, the Market is the city's the most popular shopping destination for local handcrafted goods. Shoppers and browsers relish the unique opportunity to meet more than 350 Northwest artists and craftspeople who create the art they're selling. An interactive map on the Portland Saturday Market website allows you to peruse all the vendors and search by product type. Live local music and myriad exotic foods top off this remarkable Saturday and Sunday event.

FESTA ITALIANA

Portland
Pioneer Courthouse Square, 701 SW 6th Avenue
Late August
www.festa-italiana.org

According to author Charles Wills in his 2005 book *Destination America*, about 25,000 Italian immigrants had arrived on American shores by 1870, largely from Northern Italy—people displaced and impoverished by the wars of unification and independence during the Risorgimento. But within a few decades, between 1880 and 1924, more than 4 million Italians immigrated to America, largely spurred on by devastating poverty in Southern Italy and Sicily. Like other immigrant groups of the time, Italians arriving in America sought opportunity for a better life and many eagerly embraced westward expansion. By

Marionettes are among the most popular attractions at lively Festa Italiana.

the early 1900s, Oregon, and Portland especially, had a burgeoning Italian population—so much so that until urban renewal in the early 1960s, Portland had a thriving Italian business district.

Today, Italian culture continues to deeply influence the city and the nation at large, from the foods we love to many everyday words and phrases. Portland's annual Festa Italiana, launched in 1991, celebrates Italian culture and heritage and its influence on America and Portland. Festa Italiana, which annually attracts perhaps thousands of people, features incredible food from local restaurants that offer their takes on dishes familiar to most Americans, to Italian regional specialties that demonstrate the amazing depth and creativity in Italian cuisine. Accompanying all the terrific foods are numerous Italian wines and beers. Nonstop entertainment at Festa Italiana features not only live musicians but also dancers and other performers, even marionette puppeteers (loved by the children who attend), all specializing in cultural expressions of the arts, for which Italy has long been known.

This spirited three-day festival also features a popular bocce competition on Sunday. Bocce, of Italian origin, is somewhat akin to lawn bowling; it has been described as a combination of bowling, shuffleboard, and Skee-Ball. One of the world's most popular games, bocce is played with eight large spherical balls, four balls per team, with each team's balls differing in color so they are distinguishable (see the Festa website to register).

Festa Italiana, which is free to attend and family friendly (21 and over for the beer and wine gardens) and envelops Downtown Portland's Pioneer Courthouse Square each August, also includes various Italian American organizations selling Italian foodstuff and other products. Opening ceremonies occur Friday at noon, followed by the popular wine-grape stomp and pizza-tossing competition. The fun lasts well into the night, with featured musicians taking the stage throughout the evening. Each day Festa Italiana runs from 11 am to 11 pm, and fills the square with buoyant crowds.

SIDEWALK CHALK ART FESTIVAL

Forest Grove
Main Street
Third Saturday in September
www.valleyart.org/chalkart/

Chalk, concrete, and sunny summer days go hand in hand. However, kids doodling on the driveway barely hints at the versatility of this medium that so many artists find appealing. Perhaps it's the wide range of chalk colors and the way they blend so seamlessly in the hands of a skilled artist. Or maybe it's the ephemeral nature of drawing on this outdoor canvas, knowing that the

Amazing artworks come to life on city sidewalks during the Sidewalk Chalk Art Festival in Forest Grove.

artwork cannot survive the rain or the hose or the shuffle of feet. Whatever their motivation and inspiration, artists of all ages and abilities flock to the Valley Arts Sidewalk Chalk Art Festival, which has transformed Forest Grove's eclectic Main Street into a giant kaleidoscopic mural each September since 1991.

Beginning at 8 am on the third Saturday of September, chalk artists take to the street, literally, to weave their beguiling magical tapestry of shapes and colors. The sidewalks are quickly transformed into beautiful works of creative expression. Anyone can take part in the fun, no matter their age or artistic skills, and this popular festival draws throngs of onlookers who enjoy watching the many different drawings taking shape throughout the day and often stroll the downtown blocks after the event to see the wonderful artwork. Kids love to get in on the action alongside many talented established artists, including a select group of featured artists announced late each summer in advance of the event.

The festival is held rain or shine, though pleasant late-summer weather frequently prevails; in the event of rain, many artists employ pop-up tent-canopies or umbrellas to forestall the inevitable as long as they can. In addition to their imaginations, artists and aspiring artists should bring knee pads, rulers, blending brushes, and any other supplies they need. The entry fee for artists is minimal, and members of Valley Art get a discount; registration fees include a tray of richly pigmented chalks and a square of Downtown Forest Grove sidewalk for the day. There is no entry fee for onlookers. Preregistration begins the Wednesday prior to the festival at Valley Art Gallery, 2022 Main Street in Forest Grove.

The event runs until 4 pm and includes ongoing entertainment suitable for all ages. It is partially funded by a grant from the community enhancement project, and proceeds from the festival help fund scholarships for Forest Grove High School students who will be continuing with their art studies in college. It also benefits the Valley Art Association's children's art classes. The Sidewalk Chalk Art Festival is noncompetitive—no art contest, no judging. It's all about the art, the community, and the camaraderie.

DOGTOBERFEST

Portland
Lucky Lab Brew Pub,
    915 SE Hawthorne Boulevard
Mid-September
www.dovelewis.org/dogtoberfest

Iconic Portland brewery Lucky Labrador Brew Pub opened in 1994, and the next year founders Gary Geist and Alex Stiles hatched the idea of Dogtoberfest for their first anniversary celebration. Then, a year later in 1996, they realized this event could be a valuable and spirited annual fundraiser, so they invited

nonprofit DoveLewis Emergency Animal Hospital to partner with them in the event as the beneficiary. This dogcentric celebration proved to be a big hit, and by the time its twentieth anniversary rolled around in 2015 Dogtoberfest volunteers had bathed about 9,000 dogs and raised nearly $200,000; and those totals keep expanding—to the tune of about $20,000 per year—as the public has warmly embraced this amusing and convivial festival held each September, usually a time of pleasantly warm late-summer dogwashing weather in the Willamette Valley.

Dogtoberfest, which includes a popular dog wash, is a terrific fundraiser for the DoveLewis Emergency Animal Hospital.

Central to Dogtoberfest, of course, is the dog wash itself: bring your four-legged buddy, invite your family, and get ready to get wet, all in the name of a great cause, as proceeds and donations go to the DoveLewis Blood Bank, which provides dogs and cats with more than 500 lifesaving blood transfusions every year. DoveLewis, established in 1973, is the region's only nonprofit twenty-four-hour emergency and critical-care and specialty animal hospital. The idea for the hospital sprung from well-known kennel owners, dog breeders, and groomers Dove and AB Lewis. Before her untimely death at age 54 in 1972, Dove Lewis and Dr. Richard Werner had hopes of establishing an overnight animal hospital but could not find financial support. But after Dove's death, her devoted husband, AB, encouraged by Werner, used money he had intended to donate as a bequest to instead open the animal hospital.

Nowadays, thanks to this wonderful collaboration between Lucky Labrador Brew Pub's founders and DoveLewis, dogs and their owners enjoy a terrific celebratory festival in the form of Portland's biggest dog wash—probably one of the biggest anywhere. In addition to dog washing, grooming, and nail trimming, attendees enjoy live music, a variety of vendors, great food, and outstanding beer—including the special Dogwash Pale Ale.

VERNONIA SALMON FESTIVAL

Vernonia
Hawkins Park
Early October
www.vernoniahandsonart.org/salmon-festival/

Though its twentieth-century calling card was logging and
lumber milling, the pretty, little, off-the-radar town of Vernonia
actually started as an isolated farming community near the Nehalem River
in the mid-1870s, founded by a handful of early settlers—Clark Parker, John
and Nancy Van Blaricum, Ozias Cherrington, and Judson Weed (for whom the
nearby town of Weed is named). They named the town Vernona after Weed's
daughter, but a clerical error during incorporation made it Vernonia. In those
days, the Nehalem River and its tributaries annually drew massive runs of
salmon and steelhead—a legacy that this close-knit community honors today
with its annual Vernonia Salmon Festival.

Each October the Salmon Festival, held at Hawkins Park, celebrates
not only the annual run of fall chinook salmon but also local agricultural,
art, and community cohesion. The Salmon Festival offers activities for all
ages and is great for children, with lots of hands-on fun: photo boards, art
projects, scavenger hunts, pumpkin carving, scarecrow making, and even
trout fishing in a special stocked pond. Moreover, one of the key sponsors

*Claudia, a key part of the Vernonia Salmon Festival, is a 20-foot-long hollow salmon
replica with interpretive displays inside.*

of the event, the Upper Nehalam Watershed Council, brings ever-popular Claudia the Chinook for kids to explore: Claudia is a twenty-foot-long hollow replica of a salmon, and inside is a hands-on educational display about salmon habitat. Children get to climb in and out of her and learn more about salmon, as well as watch the real thing—live chinook salmon back from the ocean to spawn—in nearby Rock Creek.

The festival grounds also host numerous vendors offering unique handmade crafts, artworks, functional wares, foods (including salmon), and more, along with nonprofits and a variety of agricultural and historical displays. Throughout the day, live music entertains attendees. Hands-On-Art, in addition to providing some of the free activities for kids, runs a raffle and cooks up delicious salmon kabobs and chowder, with proceeds benefiting an arts scholarship at Vernonia High School.

Straddling both the Nehalem River and Rock Creek, Vernonia sits north of US Highway 26 and south of US Highway 30, both of which reach the Oregon Coast. Connecting them, State Route 47—the Vernonia Highway—leads to this attractive town of 2,300 people set amid bucolic farmlands and verdant forestlands about forty miles northwest of the Portland metro area. It's just far enough off the major highways to maintain a wonderful small-town ambiance.

HP LOVECRAFT FILM FESTIVAL® & CTHULHUCON

Portland
Hollywood Theatre, 4122 NE Sandy Boulevard
Early October
www.hplfilmfestival.com/hplfilmfestival-portland-or

Though his works are deeply appreciated in literary criticism and popular culture today, Howard Phillips ("HP") Lovecraft (1890–1937) never achieved notoriety for his enrapturing horror fiction, published only in pulp magazines in the 1920s and '30s, during his oft-troubled lifetime. He died at age 46, and nearly three decades more would pass before a broader audience discovered his riveting, creative, oft-bizarre horror stories, such as "The Colour Out of Space," "The Rats in the Walls," and "The Call of Cthulhu," which opens with the memorable and poignant—and very Lovecraftian—

line: "The most merciful thing in the world, I think, is the inability of the human mind to correlate all its contents."

And correlating enthralling content is the privilege of attendees at Portland's HP Lovecraft Film Festival, which annually invites a cadre of the best professional and amateur independent filmmakers to submit

A variety of memorabilia from the HP Lovecraft Film Festival.

their creepiest, scariest, weirdest movies. Each year, the festival screens nearly three dozen films—full-length movies and short films alike—that revel in the bizarre, spooky, mysteries, and macabre. The lineup of films is announced each year and the filmmakers who have earned their way onto the festival screen at Portland's historic (and reputedly haunted) Hollywood Theatre produce such petrifying works of Lovecraftian horror that many of the best are even available each year on "Best of" DVD collections funded by an annual Kickstarter campaign.

Of course the carefully selected lineup of independent movies is the highlight of the HP Lovecraft Film Festival, but this event is more than a film festival; it is a celebration of Lovecraft, his work, and the genre of horror fiction he helped create and define. In addition to film screenings, the festival brings in intriguing guests, holds panel discussions and special readings, hosts a variety of vendors, and sometimes even presents live music. With its screenings typically sold out (advance ticket purchase is wise), the festival attracts a broad audience and is organized and hosted by the same people who produce Portland's exceptional and popular Horror Film Festival each spring. Together, the HP Lovecraft Film Festival and the Portland Horror Film Festival (see page 28) annually give fright-film fans chills and thrills enough to last... until the next year.

THE WEDGE

Portland
Portland Night Market, 100 SE Alder Street
Early October
www.thewedgeportland.com

In the earliest years of Westward expansion, immigrants to the Oregon Territory realized the propensity for raising dairy cows in the temperate climate and bucolic valleys west of the Cascade Mountains. The first dairy cows arrived in the Tillamook Valley in the early 1850s, and by the early 1890s, the state had enough commercial dairies to necessitate founding the Oregon Dairy Farmers Association (ODFA). Commercial cheese production lagged behind the production of butter, milk, and cream, but the state's now-robust cheese industry got a major boost when Canadian Peter McIntosh moved to the Tillamook Valley in 1894 at the behest of two local small-production cheesemakers. McIntosh realized the isolated valley was better suited to cheese than butter—cheese could better withstand delays in transportation than butter, which easily spoiled in the days before refrigeration. By 1900, Tillamook County boasted some three dozen creameries producing cheese, and the industry had likewise burgeoned in other parts of Western Oregon.

More than 100 years would pass before the state's cheesemaking industry founded its own statewide lobby and support organization with the launch of the Oregon Cheese Guild (OCG) in 2006. Among the guild's goals is to support and promote Oregon's artisanal cheesemakers alongside Oregon's large creameries, and as such, OCG created the Oregon Cheese Trail and founded two outstanding cheese festivals—the Oregon Cheese Festival in Southern Oregon, and The Wedge in Portland.

The Wedge is a culinary delight for all ages—it's a farmers'-market-style

A cheesemonger plies his craft at The Wedge, a celebration of craft cheeses.

event featuring a staggering array of different cheeses from creameries big and small, along with many other foods and beverages. Attendees can sample and purchase Oregon artisan cheeses, enjoy intriguing specialty foods, and wash it all down with a craft ale, Oregon wine, or regional cider. More than sixty vendors attend The Wedge annually. The art of the cheesemonger is on full display, not only with the copious and varied cheeses available but also with the deft handling on various cheese knives, such as the boska and various incarnations of the double-handled mezzaluna, to precisely cut wedges from weighty cheese rounds, or "wheels."

Those cheese wheels, in fact, are the star attractions in the hilarious cheese-wheel bowling at The Wedge, one of a variety of all-ages activities. Attendees can also embrace the educational side of cheese through a variety of special Master Classes held each year and taught by local experts. Classes cost a bit extra, and admission to The Wedge is around $20 in recent years, with tickets going on sale in August (advance purchase earns a discount and is a wise move given the popularity of the event). Tickets include a discount voucher for purchasing a favorite offering from one of the many vendors. The Wedge also offers wine-flight tickets, which include a commemorative glass and samples of not only wine, beer, and ciders, but also locally produced spirits, mead, and even saké.

The Wedge runs from 11 am to 5 pm on Saturday, and actually kicks off a week earlier with a special Cheesemakers Dinner featuring five Oregon creameries whose cheeses are integrated into each of five courses. For details and ticket information, visit the event's website. The festival venue, Portland Night Market, is a popular indoor venue about two blocks east from the east foot of the Morrison Bridge. Parking can be tricky, so consult The Wedge website for suggestions.

KILLER PUMPKIN FESTIVAL

Portland
Rogue Eastside Pub, 928 SE 9th Avenue
Late October
www.rogue.com

Oregon craft brewers proved long ago that their ingenuity has few bounds—almost anything edible has found its way into "the boil," so to speak, and the result has been several decades of ales bearing flavors all across the spectrum, from sweet to savory and every iteration in between and beyond. Pumpkin is a natural choice in more ways than one: Northwest brewers are relative latecomers to the pumpkin beer concept, but for as far back as colonial times, brewers in New England realized that pumpkins— an indigenous and abundant squash that the Native Americans had cultivated for centuries—were ideal for making beer in the relative absence of barley malt. Pumpkin meat had fermentable sugar, whereas the traditional malt was in short supply in the colonies. It was invention by necessity.

No Portland October would be complete without a visit to the Rogue Killer Pumpkin Festival.

Modern incarnations of pumpkin beers run the gamut from subtle nuance to a mouthful of liquid pumpkin pie, and range from light ales to high-octane barrel-aged expressions. Moreover, they are practically legion, and Rogue Brewery's Killer Pumpkin Festival showcases dozens of Northwest pumpkin beers just in time for the Halloween season. This one-day mini–beer fest focuses specifically on the wonderfulness of turning pumpkins into beers, and the event is family friendly (21 and over to drink, of course), with Rogue providing a bunch of actual pumpkins to bowl, decorate, carve, and smash, along with costume contests for kids, adults, and even dogs. In fact, kids love the activities, with the pumpkin smash perhaps being the odds-on favorite (among kids and adults). Proceeds from Killer Pumpkin Fest entry donations benefit Camp Ukandu (www.campukandu.org), whose mission is to bring joy and hope to children living with cancer, their siblings, and their families through fun camp experiences.

Rogue's Eastside Pub (which many Portlanders remember as The Green Dragon prior to 2017) whips up a special pumpkin-inspired menu for the event, providing a chance for ale aficionados to pair pumpkin beers with pumpkin foods; and you don't want to miss the tapping of the pumpkin "keg" full of beer—a tradition at the Killer Pumpkin Fest. This zany good time also features a variety of vendors, live music, and even pumpkin ice cream. Of course the heart and soul of Killer Pumpkin Fest is the lineup of pumpkin beers: love 'em or hate 'em, they are a blast to try and vary considerably in flavor and style. Each year the event's beer menu includes concoctions from a who's who of area breweries.

PORTLAND BOOK FESTIVAL

Portland
Portland Art Museum and other venues
Early November
www.literary-arts.org/what-we-do/pdxbookfest/

Oregon's premier literary festival, the Portland Book Festival (nee Wordstock) annually gathers more than 100 authors whose most recent books have impressed festival planners enough to select them from among countless applicants for participation in this prestigious, multifaceted event sponsored by Literary Arts. Based at the Portland Art Museum in Downtown Portland, with neighboring venues hosting a variety of activities, this popular festival features numerous author events for the public, writing workshops, youth activities, pop-up readings, an extensive book fair with dozens of vendors, live music, local food trucks and beverage garden, and more.

The lineup of attending authors is announced in early September after an arduous selection process. Featured authors—from the Northwest and beyond—range from well-known established veterans with myriad titles to their credit, to writers who have recently enjoyed publication of their first book.

Authors chosen to appear represent a variety of fiction

Portland Book Festival, held at the Portland Art Museum, is Portland's premier literary event.

and nonfiction genres, and they participate in onstage discussions, interviews, question-and-answer sessions, and readings throughout this bustling one-day event. Tickets to the festival—less than $20 in recent years—are available in advance (recommended) via the Literary Arts website, www.literary-arts. org, and at the door, and include access to all festival events, including the massive book fair, and to the Portland Art Museum. Attendees age 17 and under are admitted for free, as are active military personal and military veterans. Significantly, at all Portland Book Festival venues and all events, entry and seating are available on a first-come, first-served basis; standing in line does not guarantee entry. The museum itself does not have a dedicated parking lot, but the downtown area has street parking and myriad parking lots and garages, as well as an excellent public transit system.

Founded as Wordstock in 2005 by Portland writer and educator Larry Colton, the Portland Book Festival draws nearly 10,000 attendees annually, yielding a wonderfully Portlandesque event right down to the inevitable food trucks parked outside the museum.

WILD ARTS FESTIVAL
Portland
Montgomery Park, 2701 NW Vaughn Street
Mid-November
wildartsfestival.org

Celebrating nature in art and literature is the central theme of the Wild Arts Festival, a colorful and educational fundraiser for the Audubon Society of Portland. This two-day extravaganza, launched in 1980, assembles an amazing diversity of artists, including painters, sculptors, jewelers, photographers, woodworkers, glassblowers, and more, all displaying and selling their works just in time for holiday shoppers looking for unique gifts for nature-loving family and friends.

Moreover, the Wild Arts Festival includes a popular book fair that features an eclectic mix of novelists, photographers, poets, children's authors, nonfiction writers, and more, all with a strong commitment to the natural world. Festival attendees can peruse and purchase new and favorite titles, as well as talk with authors and have them sign their books.

Among the festival highlights is the 6x6 Wild Arts Project, which showcases some 200 unique works of donated bird-theme art, each existing within a six-inch-square space. These small gems sell out fast, with all proceeds supporting the conservation, environmental education, and wildlife rehabilitation work of the Portland Audubon Society. Festival regulars know to line up early to get first dibs on this exhibit. Anyone can donate art

Wild Arts Festival draws together an amazing collection of talented artists and their works.

to the 6x6 project—the art materials are donated (see the event website for details on how to participate). The Wild Arts Festival also includes a popular silent auction that annually includes well over 200 special items, including unique artworks (to donate, see the event website).

Established more than a century ago with a mission to promote the enjoyment, understanding, and protection of native birds, other wildlife, and their habitats, the Audubon Society of Portland connects people with nature and their power to protect it. The chapter, which has about 13,000 members, maintains the 150-acre Audubon Nature Sanctuary just five minutes from Downtown Portland. The Wild Arts Festival, made possible by more than 200 volunteers, provides critical funding for the organization.

HOLIDAY ALE FESTIVAL

Portland
Pioneer Courthouse Square,
   701 SW 6th Avenue
Early December
www.holidayale.com

The Pacific Northwest is so beercentric that general brew festivals don't entirely sate the erudite cerevisaphiles (to use beer writer Gregg Smith's term for beer enthusiasts), hence the proliferation of events celebrating specific types of beer, in this case the broad category of winter ales. At the Holiday

Ale Festival, which appropriates Pioneer Courthouse Square in Downtown Portland for five days in early December, dozens of special holiday ales—all available for sampling—represent myriad regional breweries.

The names alone are invocative of the holiday spirit, with past samplings including such creative monikers as Papa Noel's Special Reserve (Alameda Brewing), Twas the Beer Before Christmas (Bear Republic Brewing), Cherry Christmas (Lompoc), Kris KrigAle (Old Town Brewing), A Tipple for Nikolaus (Zoiglhaus Brewing), and—naturally—Keg Nog, by Burnside Brewing. Naughty or nice, the weather is kept at bay by huge clear-top tents that provide attendees a view of the nearby city lights and the giant Christmas tree that adorns the courtyard annually.

To enter and taste beers, attendees must purchase an initial tasting package (in advance online or at the door), which includes a souvenir glass and a select number of beer tickets (cash only). Additional beer tickets are available for a nominal fee. Previous years' mugs/glasses cannot be used and will not be filled; however, current year glasses can be reused on subsequent visits within the same yearly festival, and the current year's mug plus a wristband allows readmission for no additional cost. Designated driver tickets are available for a modest fee.

Each year the festival includes a Sunday Beer Brunch, which requires purchase of a special ticket and features a fantastic European brunch menu and a selection of unique ales. Tickets routinely sell out soon after they go on sale, so check the event website well in advance. Parking is challenging in the area, so use the downtown parking garages and public lots, or park remotely and use the MAX line, which stops at Pioneer Square.

Holiday Ale Festival caps the Portland beer fest season with a big exclamation point.

WILLAMETTE VALLEY AREA FESTIVALS

WILLAMETTE VALLEY AREA FESTIVALS

Oregon's fertile Willamette Valley attracted many of the West's first settlers from back east—they came here in the opening decades of the nineteenth century, beginning not long after Lewis and Clark pioneered the way. Most came for the temperate climate, ideal for farming, and a variety of festivals celebrate the region's agricultural heritage as well as its cultural diversity.

The Willamette Valley technically includes the Portland metro area, but with the bulk of the state's population residing in the Portland area and a substantial number of Oregon's festivals held there, it warrants its own section in the book. What remains is a sizeable geographic area stretching from the southern edge of the Portland metro area south more than 100 miles. The valley is home to Oregon's second- and third-largest cities, Salem and Eugene respectively, and an intriguing array of small communities, some of them quietly tucked into the low hills ringing the valley. Some of Oregon's most joyous and entertaining festivals occur in these small towns, and the larger cities host an intriguing mix of major festivals that draw huge crowds and small events that provide that I've-found-a-guarded-secret feeling to festivarians.

State highways and secondary roads branch off I-5 or depart major towns to reach into and beyond the foothills; navigating the Willamette Valley en route to festival events is easy, and parking at your destination ranges from downright frustrating at times in places like Downtown Salem, to surprisingly easy. All the major communities in the valley expertly cater to visitors; after all, two of them—Eugene and Corvallis—are home to major universities, and another—Salem—is the state capital.

Salem, Eugene, and Corvallis are fun cities. Eugene's variety of small districts are fun to explore; Corvallis has a wonderfully rejuvenated downtown area (revitalized quite some time ago and thriving today); and Salem quietly offers an underappreciated downtown area that begs exploration on foot, especially for food and drinks. And of course each small town out in the countryside offers its own charm; some communities boast well-known attractions (Oregon Gardens in Silverton, for example), while others offer little-known treasures in the form of restaurants, breweries, pubs, shops, historical sites, museums, and more.

OREGON TRUFFLE FESTIVAL

Yamhill Valley and Eugene
Various venues
Late January to mid-February
www.oregontrufflefestival.com

There's a lot more to a truffle than meets the eye—but an eye meeting a truffle is a troublesome affair, at least when the beguiling little fungi remains in situ. Truffles are the most coveted of Oregon's many wild mushrooms, the most coveted in the world, in fact. But they don't come easily because these roundish mushrooms do not grow above the surface of the soil. Finding these delectably earthy-tasting prizes requires an animal with a nose for the task; pigs have been used for centuries in Europe to find truffles, but dogs have largely replaced them. Without a truffle dog, finding these treasured mushrooms requires ample knowledge and then plenty of luck in searching likely areas by gently raking away the duff layer atop the soil—and doing so with a deft touch so as not to damage immature truffles or their habitat.

In North America, Oregon is at the forefront of the truffle experience, with both Oregon white truffles and Oregon black truffles, as well as the more recently identified Oregon brown truffle, considered the culinary equals of the truffles of Europe. Moreover, Oregon is home to the first truffle festival in the English-speaking world. Each winter in late January—a time when truffle hunters take to the field, guarding their secret hotspots with the utmost care—the Oregon Truffle Festival offers ten days of intriguing, educational, and mouthwatering events in both the Yamhill Valley and in Eugene and the Southern Willamette Valley. From award-winning chefs to truffle industry experts to food journalists and food enthusiasts, dozens

Oregon Truffle Festival celebrates one of the sumptuous wonders of the natural world.

of renowned culinary personalities and industry players participate in the Oregon Truffle Festival every year. It's the only event of its kind in the country. This is an international event that joins truffle fanciers and truffle experts from all over the world in celebration, educational seminars, and hands-on experiences. Moreover, the Oregon Truffle Festival also includes the fascinating Joriad™ truffle dog championships.

Each year, more than a dozen special events comprise this celebration of every aspect of these enchanting fungi. The specific events change to some extent annually, assuring that multiyear attendees will always find something new. Many events are packaged into all-inclusive multiday master classes that include expert speakers, outstanding meals prepared by world-class chefs, actual truffle hunting, tremendous camaraderie, and more. The full multiday packages in both the McMinnville area and the Eugene area cost several hundred to about $1,000 per person (depending on specific package) and include the incredible culinary experiences. A la carte tickets are available for some of the events within the packages. These culinary events sell out quickly each year, so whether you prefer a la carte tickets or full three-day all-inclusive packages, get tickets as soon as they go on sale via the festival website.

Among its myriad activities, the Oregon Truffle Festival includes the Truffle Growers' Forum, an annual gathering and focal point for the North American truffle cultivation industry. It attracts an international cast of speakers and growers from across the continent to discuss the breadth of thought and methods employed by successful truffle producers throughout the world. The Truffle Growers Forum is available as a two-day a la carte event or as a full-weekend package.

For both the diehard truffle-aholic and the casual attendee looking for a low-cost, educational, product-rich event, the Oregon Truffle Festival also offers a Fresh Truffle Marketplace during both festival weekends. This signature event provides a unique tasting and demonstration experience that brings together fresh ripe Oregon truffles, regional wines, artisan foods, and craft products and services related to the burgeoning regional truffle industry as well as the local farm and forest to table bounty. The Fresh Truffle Marketplace offers fresh native truffles for sale, truffle cooking demonstrations, a truffle dog demonstration, and an all-day lecture series.

SALEM WINTER BREWFEST

Salem
Oregon State Capitol Building, 900 Court Street NE
Early February
www.salemwinterbrewfest.com

Oregon's capital city has rapidly embraced the early-February Salem Winter Brewfest as much for the 100 or so beers available for tasting as for the unique location: directly across the street from the Oregon State Capital building. The four-day event fills a huge heated tent and features all the local breweries plus many more from around the Northwest. For quite a few years, Salem's craft brewery scene lagged behind that of Portland to the north and Eugene to the south, but it has been gaining ground since, with a cadre of excellent brewers dispersed around the city.

The breweries all generally show up to pour their latest beers at the Salem Winter Brewfest, which also features local food vendors providing superb fare to accompany a pint of your favorite craft brew. Live music every evening of the festival features regional bands and soloists performing on a large central stage. Tickets, available by the day, for two days, or for the entire weekend, are available at the door, at local taphouses and breweries, and online through the festival website. Additional sample tokens are available for purchase at the event.

The festival kicks off on Wednesday evening and runs until 10 pm, and runs from 4 to 10 pm on Thursday, then 11 am to 11 pm both Friday and Saturday. Often, until the Friday and Saturday crowds burgeon, street-side parking is available close to the festival tent. Otherwise, parking is available at the underground Capitol Mall parking structure directly below the event site from 7 pm to midnight Wednesday through Friday and 10 am to midnight on Saturday

Salem's Winter Brewfest draws congenial crowds and a host of excellent local ales.

(access to the structure is on Chemeketa Street and the gates are locked promptly at midnight). The downtown area also has several public parking garages.

KLCC BREWFEST

Eugene
Lane Events Center, 796 W 13th Avenue
Mid-February
www.klcc.org

Awash in the yellow and green school colors of the University of Oregon, Eugene is a vibrant, active, intriguing city offering all kinds of pleasant diversions, from cheering on Ducks football amid a sea of fans at Autzen Stadium to canoeing the Mill Race on a sunny summer day. The city offers a thriving university district with intriguing museums, world-class libraries, lively bars, and fun restaurants. Eclectic eateries, popular breweries, and diverse shops await visitors to the city's downtown core and nearby districts.

Eugene loves its craft beers, and like all of the Willamette Valley, the city absorbs its fair share of rainfall— and those two circumstances make February the perfect time for a lively, monumental, indoor beercentric party: the annual KLCC Brewfest captures the city's spirited energy in one great big show floor at the Lane Events Center. KLCC (89.7 FM), based at Lane Community College, is a community-supported noncommercial public radio station and a charter member of NPR. Each year the radio station assembles an incredible lineup of local and regional brewers—about eighty in total—along with both DJ-coordinated and live music for its largest fundraising event.

Rogue Ales are among the many standouts at the popular KLCC Brewfest.

The KLCC Brewfest emphasizes specialty and seasonal brews, so attendees enjoy copious opportunity to sample many limited-production and unique ales. Attendees get to vote for their favorite beer in the People's Choice award competition. The event also features a special "Collaboration Brew," in which all the local brewers collaborate in the fall and decide on one style of beer they will each produce just for the KLCC Brewfest; these special nanobrews are then available for sampling at a dedicated booth at the festival.

A modest daily (or two-day) fee gains entry to this grandiose brew fest, and three-ounce beer samples cost $1 each, with upwards of 200 different beers available. Tickets are available in advance on the festival website and at the door. This 21-and-over-only event closes at 11 pm each night. Abundant free parking space is a major plus at the Lane Events Center, as is the free one-day bus pass available for the event from Lane Transit District (LTD), allowing attendees to get to and from the festival from anywhere in the city.

WURSTFEST

Mount Angel
Mount Angel Festhalle, 500 S Wilco Highway
February or March (always the Friday/Saturday
    prior to Ash Wednesday)
www.mtangelwurstfest.org

Wurstfest

From the heart of the Willamette Valley into its foothill fringes, February promises the first blooming crocuses and daffodils thanks to Western Oregon's temperate climate—and late winter also hails the arrival of the Mount Angel WurstFest, which provides ample proof that Oregonians love to celebrate the innocuous and the enjoyable, whether it be activity, heritage, product, or—in this case—meat products in the form of German sausage. Always held the weekend prior to Ash Wednesday in the beautifully appointed, German-themed community of Mount Angel, WurstFest is like a miniature Oktoberfest all held under one roof (and of course Mount Angel is the scene of the Northwest's largest Oktoberfest each autumn).

This jubilant celebration features lively nonstop music performed by local and regional artists, expert German dance troupes, local craft ales along with German beers, both German and local wines, arts and crafts vendors, and a variety of specialty foods. And then there are the wursts—aka the sausages;

lots and lots of sausages. Germany is synonymous with sausages, and varieties are legion. The best known is the bratwurst, typically made from pork, but sometimes from veal or beef; white sausages, or weisswursts, are fairly well known outside of Germany as well. But there are many other wursts, dozens of them, some hardly known beyond the regions in Germany where they come from.

A wurst, a pint of ale, and good times aplenty at Wurstfest in Mount Angel.

Be sure to arrive with an empty stomach and a hearty appetite because the real secret of Mount Angel's WurstFest is that all the sausages are handcrafted by local and regional specialists, and each year they supply almost two dozen different styles of wurst—bratwurst and weisswurst, of course, but also currywurst, bierwurst, fricadelwurst, smoked wursts, and many others. Buy your favorite, try something new, wash it all down with a great beer or wine.

Held at the Mount Angel Festhalle in all its Germanic splendor, WurstFest includes more than a dozen local and regional artisans and craftspeople proudly displaying their foods, condiments, hats, clothing, and more, all for sale to enjoy at WurstFest or to take home and enjoy later. Family friendly (21 and over only to drink wine and beer), WurstFest also features the Wurst 5k and Wurst 10k fun runs on Saturday morning (don't be surprised to see some runners bedecked in thematic costuming). The festival runs from 10 am to 10 pm both Friday and Saturday.

SIP! MCMINNVILLE WINE & FOOD CLASSIC

McMinnville
Evergreen Aviation and Space Museum,
   500 NE Captain Michael King Smith Way
Early March
www.sipclassic.org

MCMINNVILLE
WINE & FOOD CLASSIC

Likely no other wine festival in the world takes place amid a collection of vintage and high-tech spacecraft and military aircraft, but with its home at the Evergreen Aviation and Space Museum, the three-day-long SIP! McMinnville Wine & Food Classic offers not only a vast, outstanding collection of regional wines and foods, but also a chance for attendees to inspect some of the world's most revered airplanes and space vessels.

Held in the Space Museum section of the compound—with a Lockheed SR-17 "Blackbird" suspended overhead—this popular festival annually assembles some eighty or so wineries, ranging from some of the best-known producers in the Northwest to small, little-known vintners whose wines are difficult to find without actually visiting the vineyards. In fact, SIP! provides one of the best opportunities in the Willamette Valley to sample small-batch wines that are hardly ever seen (or never seen) on a store shelf. A select handful of regional distillers and local breweries offer alternatives to the copious and superb collection of wines available by the sample and the glassful (and by the bottle or case to take home).

Moreover, SIP! offers one of the largest and most diverse food selections of any regional winefest event, with about three dozen food specialists offering everything from local lunch and dinner specialties to sumptuous snacks and divine deserts. Some of the area's top chefs are on hand to demonstrate their techniques and discuss culinary topics with attendees. The event also features a robust assemblage of artists, craftspeople, and other businesses.

This eclectic, longstanding festival—launched in 1993—now draws more than 7,000 attendees, and, perhaps best of all, it remains an all-volunteer-produced fundraising event to benefit the children of Saint James School in McMinnville. General one-day admission

Sip! is held at a unique venue; where else can you sample wine and food amid classic warbirds?

tickets and three-day passes remain modestly priced and are available in advance via the event website or at the door; a small parking fee (cash only) allows you to park onsite. Conveniently the festival offers free parking and shuttle service from the Chemeketa College parking lot and the Civic Parking Lot behind City Hall (on First Street), and shuttles run regularly throughout the event from the city's hotels. SIP! begins on Friday afternoon and runs until 9 pm. Saturday hours are noon to 9 pm, and Sunday hours are noon to 6 pm. Friday night has become especially popular with local residents, who show up in droves, with the first 1,000 attendees receiving a free festival wineglass with paid admission.

OREGON AG FEST

Salem
Oregon State Fairgrounds, 2330 17th Street NE
Last full weekend in April
www.oragfest.com

A fun and family-friendly educational festival, Oregon Ag Fest celebrates what so many of us take for granted—where our food and clothes and other everyday items come from. Agriculture is one of the few industries that affects everyone, and while Oregon farming and ranching enjoys a rich heritage and is indeed all around us just beyond city borders, many people don't know much more than where to buy the products they need.

So Oregon Ag Fest was created to help better educate the public about the importance of agriculture through many different demonstrations, hands-on activities, and exhibits aimed at showing attendees—nearly 20,000 annually—such things as where the food they eat comes from, how sheep are raised for the wool to make clothing, the importance of our forests for ecology and human survival, and a great deal more. This two-day event features all kinds of fun activities that kids find especially joyous. In fact, the more than two dozen hands-on activities at "Ag Country," set up to reflect a rural town, are the heart and soul of Oregon Ag Fest. Plant seedlings, sample Oregon-made products, make a dirt baby, shuck corn, dig potatoes, watch chicks hatch, and choose from an array of other activities that make learning about life on the farm fun. All activities are free of charge. Kids also love the agricultural scavenger hunt.

The festival also includes a petting zoo; sheep-shearing demonstrations occur throughout the weekend; llamas parade around the ring during the annual llama show. Pony rides are among the most popular events at Ag

Oregon Ag Fest includes numerous activities that children love.

Fest, with children waiting in line by the dozens to take their turn, and the miniature pedal tractors are also a riot, as kids pick their favorite tractor and peddle an indoor obstacle course.

Ag Fest offers plenty for adults as well as kids, including a farm equipment show that draws onlookers of all ages there to see a wide array of both modern and antique tractors, combines, and other machinery. And a farmers'-market-style vendor section features many different Oregon-made goods, including foods, crafts, landscaping plants, and more. Cooking demonstrations, live music, and various stage acts occur throughout the weekend.

The festivities begin on Saturday morning from 8:30 to 10:30 with the hearty Oregon Ag Fest breakfast, which costs less than $10 per person and with all proceeds going to benefit 4-H youth programs. Parking is free and plentiful at the Oregon State Fairgrounds in Salem.

OAKRIDGE TREE PLANTING FESTIVAL

Oakridge
Various venues
Early May
www.oakridgewestfirtreeplantingfestival.com

Surrounded by the verdant forests of the Cascade Mountains, Oakridge serves as a jump-off point for outdoors enthusiast of many stripes, including mountain bikers, hikers, anglers, hunters, and more. Those conifer-shrouded slopes are the big draw, and not just for recreation: at its heart, Oakridge is a logging town that thrived in the earliest days of timber harvest in the

The Oakridge Tree Planting Festival includes a homegrown parade coursing through town.

Cascades. It didn't take long for the timber industry in the region to realize that to be sustainable, it needed to replant. Harvested trees needed to be replaced, and back in the early 1950s, Oakridge launched its annual Tree Planting Festival as a celebration of the then-booming timber industry and everything it meant to the community.

The tradition has continued all these years—since 1953—even while the forest products industry in the area is no longer the juggernaut it was then. But this popular, joyous, multifaceted festival continues, bigger and better than ever, and remains, as always, a heritage event that aims to foster community cohesion and pride, and a sense of local history. Locals can embrace their heritage; outsiders can learn what makes the area so special.

The Tree Planting Festival offers numerous activities and events for kids and adults alike. Naturally, planting trees is a major part of the festivities: each year, the Tree Planting Festival Committee takes suggestions from members of the community about locations in the Oakridge region where trees need to be established. The committee then consults with community and regional government and environmental organizations in making a final decision to select the area for the festival's tree planting activity. Be sure to bring your favorite planting tool and gloves for some hands-on, pay-it-forward fun.

A major draw of the weekend, the Tree Planting Festival Grand Parade courses through Oakridge beginning midmorning on Saturday, delighting the throngs of onlookers lining the route. Major stars in the parade and throughout the event are the Tree Festival Queen and her court, selected during the Queen Coronation and Talent Show Friday evening at the Oakridge High School auditorium. Among the other events is the Mini Olympics held at the Middle Fork Ranger District, where children from preschool up to fourth grade participate in running, jumping, and throwing contests. And both kids and adults can run or walk the annual Salmon Run on Sunday, with both a 10K run and a 3K run/walk. Both events start and finish at the Oakridge Pioneer Museum.

The Tree Planting Festival also features a quilt show, dinner theater, chicken BBQ, and a big Arts, Crafts & Entertainment Fair, with all kinds of great vendors and activities, that runs Saturday and Sunday at Oakridge Elementary School. With all the events and activities, the Tree Planting Festival will keep you busy, but be sure to carve out time to explore the community, including the wonderfully restored historic downtown district.

SHEEP TO SHAWL

Salem
Willamette Heritage Center, 1313 Mill Street SE
Mid-May
www.willametteheritage.org/sheep-to-shawl

Creating clothing and other items from the wool of sheep and other animals has helped shape human societal evolution since the end of the last ice age, and since 1985 the Sheep to Shawl festival in Salem has provided an intriguing and detailed look at the traditional processes of turning wool fiber into textile products—one of the world's most historically significant crafts.

This highly educational late-spring event, held at the Willamette Heritage Center, features numerous textile artists and craftspeople demonstrating wool fiber processing, from shearing sheep (and llamas and alpacas and even the occasional rabbit) to carding and then spinning wool, to dying it different shades, to creating products by weaving, knitting, rug hooking, and other crafts. Expert fiber artists demonstrate every step of the process and answer questions, while historical displays, such as rope making, Dutch oven cooking, butter making, and traditional blacksmithing at an operating forge, provide a realistic glimpse into the pre-industrial world and the innovative pioneer spirit. The entire family-friendly event is free to the public and includes live music, live animals, children's activities, and more. Attendees can even shop for textile products made by the expert demonstrators and other local artists.

Both the venue and the festival celebrate Salem's Thomas Kay Woolen Mill, established in 1889 amid strong support from the business community who raised $20,000 in just three weeks to help secure the mill for Salem. Early in its operation, the mill employed one in every five nonagricultural workers in Salem. The mill operated on the gravity principle, and its machinery was all run by waterpower. Fire broke out in December of 1895, burning the main building to the ground. The community rallied again to fund its reconstruction, and within six months the mill was operating again; it produced the first bolt of worsted goods west of the Mississippi in November, 1896. The mill ran continuously, through the prosperous times of the Alaskan Gold Rush and during the thin times of the Depression, surviving a single worker strike, before finally closing entirely in 1962, primarily due to competition from manmade materials like polyester.

The old Thomas Kay Woolen Mill is now the centerpiece of the five-acre Willamette Heritage Center campus, which includes fourteen historic structures with permanent and changing exhibits, a research library and archive, textile learning center, café, retail shops, art galleries, and cooperative artist studios. The entire campus is open during Sheep to Shawl, with guided interpretive tours at the historic houses.

Sheep to Shawl offers an intriguing look at the craft of processing wool.

MCMENAMINS UFO FESTIVAL

McMinnville
Hotel Oregon, McMinnville Community
   Center, and other venues
Mid-May
www.ufofest.com

Whether its cosmic or comedic—or both—the annual UFO Festival in McMinnville is one of the largest such festival in the country, second only to the massive event held in Roswell, New Mexico. This multiday event in mid-May is centered at McMenamins Hotel Oregon, and has its roots in a famous UFO sighting near McMinnville in 1950. On May 11 of that year, Paul and Evelyn Trent reportedly saw what they deemed to be a UFO; Paul ran inside their house to retrieve a camera. On June 8, two of his photos were splashed across the front page of the local newspaper, the *Telephone Register*, accompanying the lead story that day, titled, "At Long Last—Authentic Photographs Of Flying Saucer[?]."

The event soon gained the attention of national media when the wire service International News Service (INS) picked up the story, and on June 26, *Life* magazine ran a story titled "Farmer Trent's Flying Saucer." Eventually, the sighting and photos were deemed a hoax by various investigators, and predictably, self-styled "ufologists" argued in turn for the authenticity of the episode and the photos; the debate continues, but largely inspired by the story, the McMinnville UFO Festival kicked off in 1999 and has grown substantially over the years.

With intellectual skepticism largely suspended for the duration of this lively and colorful event, over the years the UFO Festival has hosted a variety of speakers— ufologists, supposed alien abductees, UFO witnesses, alien abduction researchers, paranormal investigators, and media personalities. Each year, the lineup of speakers is

Cosmic or comedic or both, the McMenamins UFO Festival is a blast.

announced in the winter and tickets to speaker events go on sale then (advance purchase is recommended, and VIP tickets are available, which include passes to all speaker events at the community center).

Free and family friendly, the festival features a variety of fun and lively events. The ever-popular Landing Party includes live music, vendors, and a beer garden; and runners of all ability levels can enter the 5K UFO Abduction Dash at Linfield College. Other favorites include the UFO Costume Parade in which people of all ages dress up in galactically inspired garb for a procession through quaint Downtown McMinnville, a pet costume contest, an Alien Costume Ball, and weekend-long free film screenings. Parking near Hotel Oregon during the UFO Festival is notoriously limited, but the city runs shuttles from numerous offsite but nearby parking areas. Otherwise, arrive early and park along the side streets, but beware the many two-hour time limit slots.

WILDFLOWER & MUSIC FESTIVAL

Eugene
Mount Pisgah Arboretum, 34901 Frank Parrish Road
Late May
www.mountpisgaharboretum.com/festivals-events

From the beautiful trilliums that signal spring's firm hold on Western Oregon to the vibrant colonies of blue camas that brighten the oak savannah, Mount Pisgah is a wildflower paradise, and Mount Pisgah Arboretum the epicenter of botany on this 1,531-foot promontory that rises high above the city of Eugene. Celebrating the incredible diversity of wildflowers not only on Mount Pisgah but throughout the region as well, Lane Community College, the Native Plant Society of Oregon, and Mount Pisgah Arboretum team up each May to produce for the annual Wildflower & Music Festival.

This popular event boasts perhaps the state's largest exhibit of wildflowers, featuring everything from commonly seen beauties to exotic-looking

Mount Pisgah Arboretum hosts a huge display of wildflowers during the annual Wildflower & Music Festival.

rarities. This enchanting, kaleidoscopic display of native flowers—and artwork—is reason enough all by itself to check out the Wildflower & Music Festival, and annually features as many as 400 species, with botanists on hand to answer questions. But this buoyant event also includes dozens of vendors selling an eclectic array of goods, including plants and flowers, arts and crafts, and many kinds of foodstuffs and ready-to-eat snacks. Throughout the day, a lineup of local bands provides music, while participants can take advantage of a variety of workshops and nature walks.

Proceeds from this family-friendly festival (a modest donation is requested for entry) support Mount Pisgah Arboretum's work in habitat restoration and environmental education. Parking is free; dogs are not allowed at the event, which runs Saturday 10 am to 5 pm. May, when the Wildflower & Music Festival is held, is prime time to explore Mount Pisgah's 17-odd miles of trails, all part of the 2,363-acre Howard Buford Recreation Area, Lane County's largest park—with Mount Pisgah Arboretum as its centerpiece.

LEBANON STRAWBERRY FESTIVAL

Lebanon
Cheadle Lake Park, 37919 Weirich Drive
First full weekend in June
www.lebanonstrawberryfestival.com

Oregon's strawberry industry got its start in 1846, when Henderson Luelling arrived from Iowa by wagon train, with two extra wagonloads of fruit and nut trees and berry plants. His berries thrived in the fertile Willamette Valley, and the first strawberry canneries opened in Oregon City in 1870, processing and shipping berries across the country. Strawberry farms sprung up throughout the valley, and in 1909—specifically to celebrate the bounty—the town of Lebanon launched what is now one of the longest-running festivals in Oregon. To this day, the Lebanon Strawberry Festival continues to honor the strawberry and celebrate the community itself.

Centerpiece of the Strawberry Festival—and the major draw for many attendees—is the famous World's Largest Strawberry Shortcake, served up by the piece to thousands of watering mouths on Saturday following the Grand Parade. Strawberry shortcake was a staple at the festival from the very beginning, but the enormous version of this flavor-packed tradition started in 1931 at Munyan Bakery, and was continued by the Shimanek's and Durlam's when they took over the bakery. These days, Mega Foods serves as the mega cake baker. The title of "World's Largest" was applied early on but has been disputed by other communities at various times. In 1975, a "Battle of the Shortcakes" pitted Lebanon against Garden Grove,

Launched in 1909, the Lebanon Strawberry Festival is one of the state's longest-running festivals.

California—Lebanon won easily with its 5,700-pound cake that served about 16,000 people. The California cake weighed a mere 1,200 pounds and served only 3,000. Just imagine the ingredient list for a 5,700-pound cake: 514 cups of sugar, 224 cups of shortening, 192 cups of eggs, 992 cups of flour, 576 teaspoons of salt, 2,048 teaspoons of baking powder, 448 cups of milk, and 18 cups of vanilla. Not to mention strawberries and giant ovens.

The strawberry shortcake (free, though donations are accepted) is served up by Strawberry Festival Court princesses after great fanfare: First, the giant cake makes its way to the festival grounds via the heavily attended Grand Parade, and once there, the reigning Strawberry Festival Queen and her court ceremonially cut the cake using an historic giant knife. Then piece after piece is passed out until it is all gone. If you have your heart set on one of those pieces of cake, make sure you arrive early—there is no telling how quickly it will get gobbled up on any given year.

Beyond the ever-popular strawberry shortcake and the flamboyantly colorful and joyous Grand Parade, the Lebanon Strawberry Festival also features the popular Junior Parade for kids of all ages on Friday afternoon— the perfect opportunity for youngsters to trick out their bicycles and wagons, or even make small floats, and feel like rock stars as they stroll down Main Street. The festival includes more than forty vendors offering an eclectic array of goods, as well as a large food court offering all kinds of edibles. The carnival section of the Strawberry Festival offers a variety of rides and fun games for all ages. Throughout the festival, which commences on Thursday afternoon, live musicians and other acts entertain crowds on two main stages. Adults 21 and over can enjoy the beer gardens as well as the late-night music that begins at 9 pm on Friday and Saturday.

The entire festival is free—there is no admission charge (a small fee is required for parking at the festival grounds). Lebanon, a friendly, close-knit community of about 16,000 people, is justifiably proud of its centenarian festival, and for Oregon festivals fans, devouring a piece of that World's Largest Strawberry Shortcake is a rite of passage.

OREGON GARDEN BREWCAMP

Silverton
Oregon Garden, 879 W Main Street
Mid-June
www.brewcampfest.com

Just outside the quaint and alluring town of Silverton, ten miles east of Salem, the popular Oregon Garden is like a zoo for plant lovers and an inspiration for home gardeners and horticulturists. Sprawling across eighty acres, this incredible tourist destination, changing with the seasons, boasts more than twenty specialty gardens: rose garden, sensory garden, water garden, wetlands, tropical house, medicinal garden, Lewis and Clark Garden, conifer garden, and many more.

Each year, the Oregon Garden hosts a variety of special events, the biggest and most popular being the annual Oregon Garden BrewCamp that draws together about forty breweries pouring more than eighty beers, as well as ciders and mead. The participating breweries come from all over, with local and regional brewers well represented. On both Friday and Saturday, live music

Oregon Garden BrewCamp is the biggest annual event held at the Oregon Gardens near Silverton.

begins at 5 pm and continues through the evening, and local food vendors offer eclectic eats.

The festival opens mid-afternoon on Friday and noon on Saturday and Sunday, and a variety of admission tickets are available for advance purchase online and at the gate. Special VIP tickets, available only by advance purchase, include three-day admission, a commemorative tasting glass, a festival T-shirt, and a number of tasting tickets. The Oregon Garden offers festival style campsites for tents, RVs, and trailers. Camping areas are all conveniently located within the boundaries of the Garden and in the middle of the festival action, just a short walk to the main stage and the beer tasting venues. Advanced online camping reservations are necessary prior to the festival. A two-night minimum camping stay (Friday and Saturday nights; up to six people per site) and purchase of a three-day festival pass for each member of your party are required.

For fest-heads who enjoy a more formal setting, the Oregon Garden BrewCamp actually kicks off on Thursday evening with an exclusive limited-space, reservations-only Brewer's Tasting Dinner at the Oregon Garden Resort. Tickets are available online for this sit-down affair that features six small-plate courses, each paired with a special beer. Onsite parking for the Oregon Garden Brewfest is available for a modest fee, and shuttles run from various parking lots in Silverton to the Gardens (the schedule is posted on the event website).

EUGENE FOOD TRUCK FEST

Eugene
Lane Events Center, 796 W 13th Avenue
    (venue can change)
Saturday of Father's Day Weekend (mid-June)
www.eugenefoodtruckfest.com

Food trucks are ubiquitous in the Pacific Northwest, having evolved from the ever-popular taco trucks that have, for years, delivered a taste of Mexican street food to Oregonians, to today's full ensemble of mobile eateries that feature every conceivable fare, from ethnic cuisine of all types to gourmet preparations seemingly more fit for a four-star restaurant.

Eugene Food Truck Fest gathers more than four dozen of the best local and regional food truck vendors in an expansive parking lot to celebrate

Arrive hungry at the Eugene Food Truck Fest, which benefits Eugene Mission.

the incredible and sumptuous diversity offered by mobile chefs and raise funds to support Eugene Mission's work on behalf of homeless people. For decades, Eugene Mission has provided a host of emergency and transitional services for homeless people with the goal of helping them once again become productive members of society.

When launched in 2016, the Eugene Food Truck Fest resonated immediately with the public: event organizers from Eugene Mission expected about 4,000 people to show up for the inaugural festival, but 13,000 people attended and helped raise $45,000. The event has been a local favorite ever since and continues to include the Eugene-Springfield area's most popular food trucks, representing a broad and eclectic array of cuisines.

Food Truck Fest is entirely family friendly and includes a kid's zone with fun games and activities for children; a modest entry fee is required for the festival (children 5 and under are free). Live music and DJs entertain the crowds throughout the day, while participating chefs compete for a celebrity-judged Eugene's Favorite Food Truck award and a People's Choice award. Growing precipitously each year, the Food Truck Fest has, in recent years, been staged at the Lane Events Center, but check the website in case the venue changes. The festival runs all day—arrive hungry!

WORLD BEAT FESTIVAL

Salem
Riverfront Park, 200 Water Street NE
Late June
www.worldbeatfestival.org

Drawing about 25,000 visitors in recent years, and with some 125 performances representing about seventy cultures, Salem's World Beat Festival celebrates multiculturalism with two full days of live music, demonstrations, children and adult activities, discussions, parades, crafts, and cuisine from around the world. World Beat transforms the capital city's expansive Riverfront Park into a kaleidoscopic wonderland with performances ranging from Australian didgeridoo to Samoan Fa'alifu Taro (coconut crème preparation), and everything in between. Artists and performers perform music and dance and demonstrate cooking and crafts from cultures all over the world.

Throughout the park, cultural activities occur in different villages—Asian Pacific East, Asian Pacific West, Americas, African, European, Native American, and World Showcase—with the villages designed to replicate idiosyncrasies and customs of cultures in those parts of the world. Each village is rich in educational opportunities for all ages. The festival offers numerous activities for children, including the popular piñata parties ongoing through the weekend.

Dining courts are located at each village, and each specializes in foods from those cultures. Festival attendees can sample from a wonderful array of international cuisine, and the festival also offers an extensive dining, wine, and beer garden. World Beat also features dragon boat races held on the adjacent slough to great fanfare. The festival kicks off Friday evening and continues from late morning until late into the night on Saturday and until midevening on Sunday.

World Beat Festival in Salem celebrates the state's diversity of cultures.

Produced by the Salem Multicultural Institute (www.salemmulticultural.org), in association with numerous local sponsors, World Beat is free to attend, but donations at the gate are encouraged. Parking is available throughout adjacent Downtown Salem, both along the streets and at several parking garages, but heed all parking signage. Saturday parking can be challenging, especially in the evening, but shuttle service is available (see the event website for details).

MCKENZIE RIVER CHAINSAW & ARTS FESTIVAL

Blue River
McKenzie Community Track & Field,
    51236 Blue River Drive
Mid- to late July
www.mckenzietrack.com/CAF

The ubiquitous chainsaw bear is iconic to the Pacific Northwest; they grace highway-side sales yards, they stand on old wooden porches on small-town markets, and they occupy corners in eclectic stores. They've been a part of Northwest culture for many years, but the bears, from rough-hewn to elaborately decorative, only hint at the depth and complexity of the chainsaw carver's art. Reputedly begun in the 1950s, chainsaw carving has blossomed into both a popular curiosity and an immensely artistic medium, and each summer, the McKenzie River Chainsaw & Arts Festival features about a dozen of the most talented artists from all around the region, gathering to demonstrate their skills and sell their wares in the verdant

A chainsaw artist roughs out a bear sculpture at the McKenzie River Chainsaw & Arts Festival.

riverside community of Blue River about forty miles east of Eugene.

Throughout this three-day event, held at the state-of-the-art McKenzie Community Track & Field complex, professional carvers work nonstop, demonstrating the deft handling of chainsaws to create a bedazzling array of sculptures, from the requisite bears to complex multipart collages, and many forms in between. In the festival's popular Quick Carve, held each day, artists transform wood into art with amazing speed and dexterity, while the Main Carve venue allows them to take their time and produce sculptures of beautiful complexity. This family-friendly festival is one of the few places where you can watch numerous artists complete sculptures from start to finish. Attendees can buy chainsaw art as well as bid on auctioned pieces, with proceeds benefitting McKenzie Community Track & Field, which provides an outstanding multi-use venue for rural community engagement, education, economic opportunities, wellness, and sports.

In addition to the carvers, a variety of craft vendors offers everything from furniture to jewelry, and food vendors keep fest-goers well sated; adults 21 and over can imbibe in beer and wine. Each year's lineup of vendors and chainsaw artists is announced on the festival website a month or more in advance. The festival also offers a Kid's Corner with many activities for children. Kids under age 12 get into the festival free; otherwise admission is just a few dollars and includes a ballot so attendees can vote for their favorite carver for the People's Choice award.

WILDWOOD MUSICFEST AND CAMPOUT

Willamina
Roshambo Artfarm, 22900 SW Pittman Road
Late July
www.wildwoodmusicfest.com

A pleasant little community on the western edge of the Willamette Valley about thirty miles northwest of Salem, Willamina traces its roots to Oregon's earliest pioneer days. The town takes its name from Ohio-born Willamina Williams (nee Craig), who arrived in Oregon with her first husband, James Maley, in 1845. Reputedly she fell off her horse and into a creek, which was subsequently named for her (Willamina Creek was first called Willamina River, a tributary to the South Yamhill River).

In the twentieth century, Willamina became a major logging town, and in its heyday, 250 logging trucks rumbled through town daily. The town's agrarian heritage is equally important, and farming remains a critical component of the local economy. Around the turn of the century, George Shoeppert established the Commercial Hotel in Willamina, creating a keystone for the burgeoning city, and more than a century later, the historic inn enjoys resurgence as Wildwood Hotel. One of its owners, Katie Vinson, joined Kim Hamblin of nearby Roshambo Artfarm in conceiving the annual Wildwood MusicFest and Campout as a celebration of regional music and of the local area.

Wildwood Musicfest is a self-sustaining event that showcases emerging artists and promotes local food and agriculture; features regional craft beers, wine, and craft cider (including ciders and wines produced onsite by Art+Science); and provides myriad free activities for kids—all while handling the environment as gently as possible. Portions of the festival proceeds go to local nonprofits. Nearly two dozen different musical acts take to the festival's single stage throughout this three-day event at Roshambo Artfarm, with the lineup announced each spring on the festival website.

Camping is available for a nominal fee in a large hayfield (no fires, no dogs, and campers must have a festival ticket). A variety of vendors provide excellent, affordable food options (along with beer and wine) with a focus on locally sourced ingredients (cash only, and there is an ATM onsite), and festival organizers go to great lengths to make Wildwood as garbage-free as possible—beverages are served in recyclable, refillable keepsake event cups available for a small fee, and flatware and plates are likewise reusable and recyclable. Three-day tickets for the entire event cost less than $100 and children under age 12 get in free; buy tickets online well ahead of time.

Wildwood MusicFest brings nearly two dozen acts to the stage near the pleasant community of Willamina.

SALEM ART FAIR & FESTIVAL

Salem
Bush's Pasture Park, 890 Mission Street SE
Late July
www.salemart.org/art-fair

SALEM ART
ASSOCIATION

One of Salem's most anticipated and beloved annual events, the three-day Salem Art Fair & Festival takes over the oak-shaded west side of beautiful Bush's Pasture Park near downtown each July and draws throngs of attendees. Many people come to peruse and purchase artworks available in countless forms from some 200 featured artists in the festival's grandiose Artist Marketplace. Most of the artists hail from the Pacific Northwest. Disciplines are sorted into myriad categories: two-dimensional mixed media, three-dimensional mixed media, ceramics, cottage crafts, digital art, drawing, emerging artist, fiber, fiber wearables, glass, graphics and printmaking, jewelry, metal works, painting, photography, sculpture, and wood.

Live music and other acts entertain the crowds on two stages, with headliner musicians taking the main stage on Friday and Saturday evenings. The main stage occupies a natural amphitheaterlike setting under a canopy of towering old-growth oaks, with food and drink booths nearby. Guests are encouraged to bring lawn chairs or blankets to sit on the grass. The family stage, meanwhile, presents a variety of acts during the day, ranging from live music to juggling to theater. Food vendors provide many culinary choices, and wine and beer gardens serve regional wines and craft beers, which you can enjoy

Attendees stroll the vendor aisles at the Salem Art Fair & Festival.

while wandering the grounds. Family friendly, the fair includes a popular Kids' Court, an area for children (and the young at heart) to use up their creative energy with a variety of artistic endeavors. Moreover, the fair itself actually kicks off at 9:30 am on Friday with a children's parade—participation is free to all kids and their families.

Entrance to the fair requires a modestly priced ticket available at the gates; children under age 12 are free, as are Oregon Trail Card holders (admission includes all stage performances, including the headline music acts). Admission is also free for everyone from 3 to 5 pm on Sunday. Hosted and organized by the Salem Art Association, the Salem Art Fair & Festival is the group's largest annual fundraiser and the largest festival of its kind in Oregon. It's also among the oldest, first launched in 1950 as the Salem Art Mart. These days the event attracts more than 30,000 visitors annually.

Parking near the fair can be challenging, especially in the afternoon and evening; limited street-side parking is available, along with limited-capacity parking lots on the north (Mission Street) and south (Leffelle Street) sides of Bush's Pasture Park. Frequently the easiest option for Saturday and Sunday is to take advantage of a complimentary HUT Portland Airport Shuttle that runs from two large downtown parking garages (325 High Street SE and 400 Marion Street NE). The shuttle runs from 10 am to 10 pm Saturday, and 10 to 6 on Sunday. Bicyclists can secure their bikes at bike corrals located near the Bush Barn Art Center Entrance on High Street and at the Leffelle Street Entrance.

HOMER DAVENPORT COMMUNITY FESTIVAL

Silverton
Downtown area and various nearby venues
First full weekend August
www.homerdavenport.com

Born near and raised in Silverton, Oregon, Homer Davenport (1867–1912)—despite no formal art training—became one of the best-known and highest-paid political cartoonists in the world, particularly after William Randolph Hearst purchased the *New York Morning Journal* in 1895, changed its name to the *New York Journal*, and assembled a handpicked staff. Hearst moved Davenport from San Francisco, where the artist had already established himself as a well-known satirical cartoonist, to New York, and soon thereafter Davenport dove wholeheartedly into the 1896 presidential election pitting Republican William McKinley against Democrat Williams Jennings Bryan. Famously Davenport made especially shrewd and frequent work of satirizing McKinley's campaign manager, Mark Hanna.

By the height of his career as a cartoonist, Davenport was earning a $25,000 per year salary—the equivalent of nearly a quarter million dollars today. But by 1905, his cartoon work was decreasing and he spent considerable time on other pursuits, including his fascination with Arabian horses (he traveled extensively in the Middle East). He authored several books, including the autobiographical *The Diary of a Country Boy* about his childhood in the Silverton area, and also worked the lecture circuit to excellent effect, his manager in that endeavor being Major James Pond, who also managed Mark Twain and Thomas Nast.

Davenport contracted pneumonia while interviewing returning survivors of the *Titanic* tragedy in New York and died soon thereafter, but he is honored each summer at Silverton's engaging Homer Davenport Community Festival, which, fittingly, includes a cartoon contest in which artists compete for cash prizes. This multiday event, often called "Homer Davenport Days" by locals, features a litany of activities and events, providing fun for all ages. Marquee attractions include the ever-colorful Homer's Parade, which courses through town to the delight of throngs of attendees lining the streets, along with the wild and whacky Davenport Races—which take advantage of the word "davenport" in its furniture form. Participants literally race via davenport—couches of all sizes mounted on wheels of some sort and peddled furiously down the racecourse, encouraged by a spirited crowd.

Vintage autos are just one part of the multifaceted Homer Davenport Community Festival in Silverton.

The festival also includes a fun run and tennis tournament, along with a ping-pong ball float fundraiser in which eager participants buy numbered balls and then all the balls are released into Silver Creek, with the first balls to reach the finish line earning prizes for their owners. Likewise, the annual dime toss is also a charity fundraiser. Throughout the festival, a burgeoning food court provides countless options and myriad vendors sell their wares at the robust arts and crafts fair. Live entertainment continues all weekend, beginning on Thursday night with the Homer Kickoff Party. Over the next three days, nearly a dozen different music acts take to the main stage with a variety of genres, from classic rock to blues to country, and more. Vintage automobiles are also part of the festival courtesy of the Flywheels Cruise-In, and both the Silverton Public Library and Silverton Historical Society offer educational and interpretive events.

Homer Davenport Community Festival is free to the public (except for race and charity event fees) and draws substantial crowds each year to its many fun and entertaining events. Parking is free at the north end of Eugene Field School at 410 North Water Street, with a continuous shuttle from there to the city park and back coming every fifteen minutes or so over the course of the weekend, starting the night before for the Kick-Off party.

WOODBURN FIESTA MEXICANA

Woodburn
Legion Park, 1385 Park Avenue
Early August
www.woodburnfiestamexicana.com

Oregon has a rich and vibrant Mexican cultural heritage, and much of the state's Mexican history is intertwined with its rich agrarian roots. The synergy of Mexican culture and Oregon agricultural development has reached its zenith in the Willamette Valley, to the point that Western Oregon—and beyond—is now a vibrant multicultural community.

For more than fifty years, the small town of Woodburn has honored Hispanic cultural heritage with the Woodburn Fiesta Mexicana, an enthralling, entertaining, and culinary-rich three-day celebration that features live music, dance performances (including traditional Mexican folk dancing and Salsa dancing), queen court, a popular and colorful parade, a huge soccer tournament (youth and adult), and even Lucha Libre (Mexican professional wrestling). The vendor lineup includes a saliva-inducing selection of Mexican food specialties that comprise a highlight of the festival. The Fiesta Mexicana Court has been a part of the festival since the earliest years, in the 1960s, and remains an integral part of the celebration. Entry to the fiesta is free on Friday (noon to 11 pm) and until 5 pm on Saturday and Sunday; thereafter, a modest entry fee is required for admission on Saturday evening (open until 11 pm) and on Sunday evening (open until 10 pm).

Woodburn Fiesta Mexicana is the state's premier celebration of Mexican cultural heritage.

Mexican heritage and culture abounds in Woodburn and surrounding communities. This city of 25,000 residents sits alongside both Interstate 5 and old Highway 99, and boasts many excellent Mexican restaurants, from sit-down dinner houses to walk-up "taco trucks" specializing in traditional street food, along with specialty markets that carry many different Mexican goods, including fruits, vegetables, spices, and other foods that are difficult to find elsewhere. In 2017, the city's famous Fiesta Mexicana was named an Oregon Heritage Tradition by the Oregon Heritage Commission, and this longstanding festival annually draws more than 20,000 people. Significantly the Fiesta Mexicana Soccer Tournament, with both youth and adult brackets, is extremely popular, so teams should register early, well ahead of the festival.

OAKRIDGE KEG & CASK FESTIVAL

Oakridge
Uptown on First Street
Mid-August
www.facebook.com/KegCaskFestival

The old timber town of Oakridge, scenically nestled in the Cascade Mountains foothills forty miles southeast of Eugene and home to about 3,200 people, suffered significantly when its mills closed in the 1980s. But such a beautiful location imbued with people dedicated to the health of their community can hardly be held down, and since those difficult days, Oakridge has undergone a steady, splendid revitalization—and one that's easy to miss if you simply pass through town on Highway 58.

Instead, discover the wonderful Uptown district: turn north off the highway on Crestview, then turn right on East First Street. Now you've reached the beautifully renovated old downtown, and there's no better time to visit that during the mid-August Oakridge Keg & Cask Festival, when East First is closed down to accommodate vendors, including a variety of regional breweries, along with wineries, cideries, and even distilleries, as well as food, crafts, and live music. Indeed, Uptown Oakridge is home to an all-cask brewery, Brewers Union Local 180, and Deep Woods Distillery, both located on First Street.

During this pleasantly congenial summertime festival, attendees wander the street, strolling among the vendors, trying new beers, and striking up conversations with complete strangers. It's a small-town vibe, a celebration of the rejuvenation of Oakridge, layered with Northwest craft beer culture that is equally at home in a diminutive mountain town as it is in the hip districts of Portland. Keg & Cask occupies a Saturday from midafternoon well

Historic Downtown Oakridge is the perfect setting for the laid-back, under-the-radar Keg & Cask Festival.

into the night, with regional bands providing live music throughout. The festival is free, with the single exception of a nominal entrance fee for the beer gardens that includes four tasting tickets (additional tastes may be purchased) and a logo tasting glass—brew-fest glass collectors can hardly consider the collection complete without this coveted addition. Proceeds from the festival benefit several local nonprofits.

Gateway to all kinds of outdoor recreational opportunities—mountain biking, hiking, fishing, and more—Oakridge (and nearby Westfir) offer several lodging options, and the Willamette National Forest, which literally surrounds the town, offers numerous campgrounds within easy reach. For all details about Oakridge, consult the Oakridge–Westfir Chamber of Commerce, www.oakridgechamber.com, and the city of Oakridge, www. ci.oakridge.or.us.

AUMSVILLE CORN FESTIVAL

Aumsville
Porter Boone Park, 1105 Main Street
Mid-August
www.aumsville.us/corn-festival-information.html

The immediate area around Salem attracted some of the Northwest's earliest wagon-train settlers in the mid-1800s. In 1863, having arrived in the Willamette Valley more than a decade earlier, Henry L. Turner purchased land from John McHaley at the future site of the small town of Aumsville, east of Salem. At the time, the settlement was called Hoggum because so many people raised pigs in the area. Turner built a flour mill on the site. Soon thereafter, however, his son-in-law, Amos Davis, died at the age of 31 (a large headstone marks his grave in nearby Turner). Henry Turner, very fond of Davis, coined the town "Aumusville" in his honor (Davis was generally called "Aumus" rather than "Amos"), which eventually became Aumsville.

Even by then the rich floodplain soils of the Willamette Valley, along with the temperate climate, had proven conducive to agriculture in many forms. Early farmers grew nearly everything—potatoes, grains, berries, greens, even fruit trees. And while the climate here is not as ideal for corn as in the nation's heartland, the state nonetheless has produced corn for both silage and consumption for generations; in 1908, in fact, the Oregon Agriculture

Experiment Station initiated a "corn improvement" program, largely aimed at creating genetic corn varieties better suited to the valley. Substantial cornfields began springing up in the Aumsville area, and to this day the area's farmers still grow lots of corn.

A vibrant corn-themed float at the Aumsville Corn Festival, held each August.

The local corn is so important to the Aumsville area that in 1969 the town hosted a modest parade for kids—the first Aumsville Corn Festival. From those humble beginnings the event evolved into a robust daylong celebration that today draws visitors from throughout the area. The fun begins with a popular parade down Main Street in Aumsville late Saturday morning, with the Corn Festival Court in attendance. Then at noon, the festivities open at the event headquarters, expansive Porter Boone Park at the west end of Main Street. Naturally, the Aumsville Corn Festival abounds in corn—more than twenty tons of the golden goodness annually in recent years.

Attendees not only could purchase corn at bargain prices, but traditionally everyone gets two ears of cooked and buttered corn for free. Moreover, both kids and adults, not to mention onlookers, love the corn-on-the-cob eating contest, and a variety of other games keep the fun rolling throughout the day— sack races, egg toss, treasure hunt, and even a keg toss. Live music entertains the crowds and vendors provide foods, crafts, and other wares; the festival even presents novelty awards to attendees in a variety of categories, such as longest distance traveled to attend. Parking is generally easy at the park or nearby within walking distance.

CARLTON CRUSH HARVEST FESTIVAL

Carlton
Wennerberg Park
Early September
www.carltoncrush.com

Oregon's burgeoning viticulture industry totals more than 700 wineries, more than 500 of them in the Willamette Valley. In such a winecentric region, festivals and other events celebrating wines and wineries are regnant, some of them massively attended and others sometimes attended by an air of hubris. But others are welcoming, relaxed, incredibly fun community celebrations, such as the wonderfully cheery Carlton Crush Harvest Festival, which perfectly epitomizes the congenial, small-town esprit of one of the prettiest and most pleasant places in Oregon's Willamette Valley wine country.

Home to about 2,000 people, Carlton and its immediate surrounds boast about two dozen wineries, ranging from small, little-known producers with cultlike followings, such as longstanding and highly reputed Carlo & Julian, to deeply respected proverbial giants in the industry, such as Ken Wright Cellars. Carlton's roots, so to speak, are decidedly agrarian, its history rich in farming and ranching. These days, of course, wine production basks in the limelight in these parts, and each September, Carlton Crush celebrates the town's ever-deepening winemaking heritage.

Especially popular at this daylong celebration are the grape-stomping events—good old-fashioned take-your-shoes-off, roll-your-pants-up, stomp-your-heart-out-in-a-big-bucket-of-wine-grapes merrymaking. The kids love it, and ages 6 through 12 get their own dedicated stomp, gooey, grapey, and purple. Later in the day, team grape-stomping

Grape-stomping events take center stage at the Carlton Crush Harvest Festival.

competitions begin to the delight of contestants and onlookers alike, with elimination rounds finally culminating in the afternoon championships. Children also enjoy the kids' watermelon-eating contests. Throughout the day, meanwhile, vendors at the Artists Market offer myriad wares, and adults can enjoy fine wines and beers produced by local and area wineries and breweries, all the while with live music providing excellent background accompaniment to the festivities. Throughout the event, terrific local restaurants offer many dining and snack choices.

Carlton Crush (no admission fee) is held at Wennerberg Park at the end of Grant Street west of downtown; free parking is available onsite and throughout Carlton within walking distance. For lodging options in and near Carlton, consult Visit Carlton, www.visitcarlton.com.

MOLALLA APPLE FESTIVAL

Molalla
Dibble House Museum Complex,
    620 S Molalla Avenue
Second Saturday in September
www.dibblehouse.org

Look carefully almost anywhere in Oregon and you might spy apple trees nearly as old as the state itself. In fact at least two still-living apple trees predate Oregon's statehood: the Haines Apple Tree in Merlin was planted in the early 1850s, and the Dorsch Yellow Bellflower Apple Tree in Portland was planted in 1850. Both are now historical treasures. In fact, Oregon was home to the first grafted-fruit-tree nursery on the West Coast, the Luelling and Meek Nursery in Milwaukie. In 1847, Henderson Luelling successfully navigated the Oregon Trail from Iowa, bringing with him not only a large family but also more than 500 young plants and trees. Settling in what is now Milwaukie, Luelling was joined a year later by his neighbor from back in Iowa, William Meek, who brought another twenty varieties of grafted trees. Their nursery thrived and Oregon's fruit tree industry was born.

Fruit trees quickly spread throughout the Willamette Valley and beyond, with apples proving especially successful, and in the mid-1850s—again, even before statehood—apple trees that survive to this day were planted on land in what is now Molalla, then owned by pioneer woman Rachel Larkin. Horace and Julia Dibble bought the parcel of land and built a house that has survived to become the headquarters for the Molalla Area Historical Society (the house was finished in 1859 and is now on the National Register of Historic Places). Those surviving apple trees are Waxen and Rhode Island Greening varieties.

Fittingly the historical society launched the Molalla Apple Festival in 1975 not only to celebrate apples in all their culinary delight but also as an educational event focusing on the settlement-era lifestyle of the 1800s. The Molalla Apple Festival features a homemade apple pie contest—pies must arrive by 11 am, as the contest begins at noon; all entrants receive a special thank-you gift. Attendees also enjoy the chance to try a variety of other baked goods, along with fresh-pressed

Apple pies lined up for the judges at the Mollala Apple Festival.

cider; in colonial and pioneer days, cider was one of the chief apple products. The festival also features vendors selling many different products. The lineup changes from year to year, but offerings typically include clothing, crafts, antiques, and more, and the museum store is open, offering books, gifts, and costumes. Throughout the day, regional musicians provide live entertainment.

The Dibble House Museum Complex features a variety of living history demonstrations and displays throughout the festival, with participants dressed in period clothing. Pioneer-era homemaker crafts, such as spinning, weaving, butter making, knitting, tatting, and bobbin lace making are shown throughout the day. Outdoors, demonstrations of cider making, panning for gold, and flint-knapping are presented.

There is no admission charge to the Molalla Apple Festival, which is a terrific event for kids as well as adults, but donations to support the museum are welcome and tax deductible. The festival runs from 10 am to 4 pm.

MOUNT ANGEL OKTOBERFEST

Mount Angel
Various venues
Mid-September
www.oktoberfest.org

Oktoberfest celebrations are ubiquitous; annually Oregon hosts perhaps a dozen or more such events at venues ranging from major cities to individual pubs.

But the Mount Angel Oktoberfest, launched in 1966, is special—a massively popular, event-rich feier (to use the German word for "celebration") that offers wonderful entertainment for all ages each September. Oktoberfest takes over the festively kept little community of Mount Angel for four days, drawing nearly 400,000 people each year. Attendance is essentially mandatory for anyone who loves festival events in Oregon.

Entertainment in the form of amazing musicians, including Bavarian and Alpine bands brought to the festival from far and wide, are a highlight of the Mount Angel Oktoberfest, taking the stage at a variety of venues. Each entertainment venue has a unique atmosphere and entertainment style. Find your favorite depending upon your mood (venue hopping is highly encouraged). Three of the venues—Biergarten, Weingarten, and Alpinegarten—require a cover charge, or simply purchase a wristband that allows admission to all three. There is never a charge for people under 21 years old, but there are slightly restricted hours in the Biergarten and Weingarten for those under 21. Biergarten is especially popular for the traditional Bavarian beers on tap, alongside special craft brewers. The Weingarten recreates the essence of a traditional Continental wine festival, with myriad wines from

The longstanding Mount Angel Oktoberfest is one of the biggest such events in the West.

both Germany and Oregon, but includes a fine selection of beers as well. Alpinegarten offers interactive entertainment for the whole family along with an excellent selection of both German and regional beers and wines.

The Prostgarten is a hidden treasure in Downtown Mount Angel, at the corner of Garfield and College Streets behind the Glockenspiel and a row of food booths. Inside the Prostgarten you will hear gentle acoustic accordion music that allows for easy conversation while you enjoy a German beer—or, rather, a "bier"—and German wines. Bring your food favorites from the outside food booths, take a seat under the tent or on the enclosed patio, have a chat with friends, and watch the crowds go by in this quiet downtown sanctuary. The other entertainment venues include the outdoor Bandstand, scene of the ever-popular Friday and Saturday night street-dance parties, and the beautiful Saint Mary's Catholic Church (built in 1912), which hosts choral groups, alpenhorn players, harp and flute music, and fine organists playing spiritual and uplifting music while guests marvel at the church's stained glass and statuary. Oktoberfest also has an extensive, fun-filled free Kindergarten for kids and families.

In addition to the entertainment venues, Oktoberfest includes a bedazzling array of foods available from numerous vendors. Naturally, Bavarian and German favorites are well represented—sausage, brauts, sauerkraut, Ruben and Berliner sandwiches, spätzle, and much more. They'll compete for your taste buds with local fare, including fish tacos, Marionberry cobbler, Russian perogies, and many typical festival foods. The food booths are run as fundraisers by a variety of local organizations, civic services, schools, churches, and clubs. The Oktoberfest website offers a map of the Alpine Food Chalets, as the food court is called (it stretches through town). Moreover, the festival includes a massive arts and crafts vendor section featuring more than 120 artisans offering all kinds of handcrafted products and Bavarian-themed products. What you won't find are commercial products or political-organization booths. Oktoberfest, by design, is a time for joy, celebration, and gemütlichkeit, the German word meaning a situation that induces a cheerful mood, of belonging and social acceptance, and unhurriedness—this is not the place for political statements or dissension.

Mount Angel Oktoberfest also provides an array of special events beyond the entertainment venues and bier gardens. Among them are a variety of footraces on Saturday, including a half marathon; classic car shows; the Sunday morning Volkswalk, a noncompetitive walking event completed at an individual's pace following a map and signage; and the hilarious and supremely popular wiener dog races held both Saturday and Sunday.

Mount Angel is rich in Bavarian culture. Many building facades are adorned with fachwerk (exposed beams), flower baskets, and wrought iron. The town boasts the Maibaum—a Tree of Trades traditional in Bavarian Villages. Don't miss the Glockenspiel, which displays the town's history rather like a large cuckoo clock. During Oktoberfest locals pull out all the stops, dirndls (festive lady's dresses) and lederhosen (men's leather pants) abound; flower wreaths in their hair, the Mount Angel School children dance the Webertanz (Weaver's Dance).

Many activities at Mount Angel's Oktoberfest are free, and only three venues require admission. Admission (for adults) is nominal, with daily passes varying slightly in price based on the day and time. The event also offers an inexpensive all-festival pass. Parking is available at two lots, one north of town and one south. Both lots are serviced by shuttles, which drops attendees at the heart of the festival and return to the parking areas about every fifteen minutes. Street parking is also available, and check the maps for handicap parking.

CLAY FEST

Eugene
Lane Events Center, 796 W 13th Avenue
Early October
www.clayfest.org

Clay is an amazingly versatile medium, equally adaptable to purely functional creations and wildly imaginative works of art. Adept artists who work with clay are bound only by their imaginations, as this long-popular form of expression can render so many different objects: tiles, jewelry, whimsical little animal forms, wall hangings, pots for plants, vases for flowers, and sculptures ranging from imitative to caricature to genres defying description. And of course clay artists produce an unlimited array of tableware—plates, bowls, platters, cups, mugs, and more.

In short, clay crafts run the gamut from primitive to exotic, and for three days each October Clay Fest in Eugene assembles an amazing and robust group of clay artists, with nearly seventy participating in recent years.

Clay Fest, held at the spacious Lane County Fairgrounds, provides a showcase for the artists and an opportunity for attendees not only to marvel at the incredible variety of clay works but also to purchase their favorite pieces or even commission something special from a favorite craftsperson. There is truly something for everyone's taste, with myriad offerings from unique and decorative to entirely functional and practical. Virtually all the artists come from throughout Oregon, with many based right in Eugene. Clay Fest is planned and run by the artists who participate in the show. A small percentage of the proceeds

Clay Fest, held in Eugene, offers artists an opportunity to display and sell their amazing works.

is used to fund the show, and the rest goes directly to the artists and to charity. The show is a fundraiser for Local Clay, an independent nonprofit organization of potters from the Southern Willamette Valley, the Central Oregon coast, and Roseburg and the vicinity. Proceeds are earmarked for the organization's Clay in Education program, which provides funding for ceramic activities in local schools.

Always a big hit at Clay Fest is the supervised Kids Clay area where children have fun creating clay pieces and gaining insights into the world of clay from the artists at the show. Another crowd pleaser is the demonstration area where some of the participating artists show how they make their work. In addition to the individual artist booths, the Clay Fest Gallery features works by participating artists, highlighting their best pieces. Gallery awards are given out for first, second, and third place, which are voted on by the potters in the show. The Lane County Fairgrounds provides abundant free parking, and admission to the show and sale is always free.

MUSHROOM FESTIVAL

Eugene
Mount Pisgah Arboretum, 34901 Frank Parrish Road
Late October
www.mountpisgaharboretum.com/festivals-events/

Oregon is home to hundreds of species of mushrooms, many of them edible, and recreational mushroom hunting has become incredibly popular, with species such as morels, chanterelles, and the state's famous truffles taking center stage. So it's no surprise that mushroom enthusiasts and people hoping to learn more about wild mushrooms flock to Eugene's beautiful Mount Pisgah Arboretum each October for the Mushroom Festival, sponsored by the Cascade Mycological Society (CMS), Mount Pisgah Arboretum, and Lane Community College.

A fundraiser for the arboretum, the Mushroom Festival features a bedazzling and voluminous display of wild mushrooms collected for the event by CMS members. Each year, the display totals more than 300 species—and in 2013, 404 species set a festival record, followed by 393 species in 2016, when collectors also managed to add a festival record 69 new species. The event hands out Best of Show awards to collectors of the most impressive individual mushrooms. Experts are on hand throughout the day to discuss everything related to mushrooms and mushroom collecting.

In addition, as live music provides ambiance, attendees (a modest donation is requested as an adult entry fee) can peruse dozens of vendor booths selling a variety of foods, including mushrooms and mushroom products, along with plants, books, crafts, artwork, and functional wares. A variety of nonprofits that support nature education and habitat restoration have educational/informational booths. Mushroom cuisine also takes center stage with culinary demonstrations featuring a variety of

Prized morels are among the numerous edible fungi that inspire the Mushroom Festival at Mount Pisgah Arboretum.

mushrooms species used in creative and delectable dishes. Additionally the Mushroom Festival offers a variety of nature walks, guided by local naturalists, on some of the many trails comprising Mount Pisgah's impressive trail network. Attendees can also enjoy hayrides, and a kids' booth features face painting and a variety of nature-oriented crafts. The event also hosts a popular scarecrow contest in which attendees vote for the winners.

Mushroom Festival runs from 10 am to 5 pm, rain or shine; dogs are not allowed. The festival offers shuttle service to the event and parking for the festival is free (see website for details). Parking at Mount Pisgah trailheads requires a Lane County parking day pass or annual pass for the Howard Buford Recreational Area (which includes the arboretum). The day pass can be purchased at the yellow vending machine next to the Mount Pisgah Summit Trailhead (on the main entrance road, uphill from the parking lots). The fee machine accepts credit and cash.

MOUNT ANGEL HAZELNUT FEST & GERMAN HOLIDAY MARKET

Mount Angel
Mount Angel Festhalle, 500 S Wilco Highway
First weekend in December
www.hazelnutfest.com

Ninety-nine percent of American hazelnuts are grown in Oregon, and the state's hazelnut industry is a world leader in hazelnut research, with Oregon State University working with the state's growers to develop new varieties that resist the destructive eastern filbert blight fungus. Hazelnuts are used for confections, including chocolates, and the nuts are pressed to create flavorful hazelnut oil. Hazelnuts, sometimes called filberts, are a primary ingredient in Nutella spread, used in Frangelico liqueur, and add a unique flavor and texture to a variety of other products.

Worth some $150 million per year in Oregon, hazelnuts rank among the state's top agricultural products—no wonder they are the star attraction in the Mount Angel Hazelnut Fest & German Holiday Market, sponsored by the Mount Angel Chamber of Commerce in cooperation with the Oregon Hazelnut Marketing Board and the Oregon Department of Agriculture. The

Hazelnut Fest's German-style holiday market includes authentic German and regional arts and crafts, Oregon wineries and breweries, and of course foods that feature hazelnuts, all under one roof at the Mount Angel Festhalle. The festival charges no admission fee, parking is free, and live music entertains the crowds throughout the event, which runs from 10 am to 5 pm on Saturday and 10 am to 4 pm on Sunday. The festivities kick off with the annual Run for your Nuts 5K road race on Saturday morning, in which runners receive hazelnuts at the finish line; for more information about the run, visit www.racenorthwest.com.

Mount Angel, a wonderful place to explore, is located in the foothills eighteen miles northeast of Salem on State Highway 214. This little town, founded in the late 1800s by German settlers, has an Old World flavor, which

is heightened by the many Bavarian-style storefronts and signage. Widely known for throwing the Northwest's largest Oktoberfest, Mount Angel, in addition to the Hazelnut Fest, also hosts an annual Wurstfest (see page 69), celebrating the renowned German sausages.

Edibles aplenty at the Mount Angel Hazelnut Fest & German Holiday Market.

SOUTHERN
OREGON
FESTIVALS

SOUTHERN OREGON FESTIVALS

Two prominent rivers that reach the ocean a hundred miles apart after long, sinuous journeys define the parameters of Southern Oregon. The Umpqua and Rogue Rivers, steeped in history, originate high in the Cascade Range before eventually leveling in their namesake valleys to provide lifeblood to agriculture, industry, and the alluring communities that make visiting Southern Oregon so appealing.

Southern Oregon comprises five counties: Douglas, Josephine, Jackson, Coos, and Curry (the latter two are coastal and are covered in the next section). Ashland anchors the southern end of the Rogue Valley. This vibrant community is renowned for its bustling arts scene that is highlighted every year by the Oregon Shakespeare Festival. Only the multilayered Portland Rose Festival draws more people. North of Ashland, the town of Medford, the Jackson County seat, basks in the sun, averaging almost 200 blue-sky days per year. Grants Pass straddles the Rogue River and is the gateway to the famous federally designated Wild and Scenic section of this rugged river. At the north end of the Southern Oregon region, Roseburg butts up against oak-covered hills that stair-step down from the Cascades in the Umpqua River drainage.

With warmer weather and longer summers than the Willamette Valley to the north, Southern Oregon vintners can cultivate wine grape varieties that produce big, bold reds. Oregon's wine industry gained its fame through pinot noirs from the Willamette Valley, but in recent years, Southern Oregon wines—merlots and cabs, Italian and Spanish varietals, dry white wines—have gained widespread accolades. Southern Oregon is also an outdoor enthusiast's mecca largely without the crowds found on the trails, rivers, and lakes of the Willamette Valley. Whitewater rafting, fishing for salmon and steelhead, hiking little-known trails, and other such opportunities abound in the region.

Fully enjoying Southern Oregon requires a commitment of time—ideally, a long weekend to take in a festival would be combined with an exploration of the area's many other attractions and activities. Along the way, expect to discover hidden gems—incredible hiking opportunities off the beaten path, boutique wineries and craft breweries few people know about, historical sites divulging intriguing details about the region's oft-tumultuous past, and of course a variety of interesting celebratory festivals.

OREGON SHAKESPEARE FESTIVAL

Ashland
Angus Bowmer Theatre, Thomas Theatre,
   and Allen Elizabethan Theatre
February through October
www.osfashland.org

The most majestic performing arts festival in the Northwest, the widely lauded Oregon Shakespeare Festival (OSF) presents nearly a dozen different plays and a host of related events ongoing from February into late October. The productions feature acclaimed directors and dozens of award-winning actors. "Inspired by Shakespeare's work and the cultural richness of the United States," says the OSF mission statement, "we reveal our collective humanity through illuminating interpretations of new and classic plays, deepened by the kaleidoscope of rotating repertory."

Each play is performed in rotating repertory throughout the festival months, and this world-class event includes several of Shakespeare's works, plays by other classic writers, as well as modern works and world premieres. The lineup for the following year's season is announced each winter. Performances are staged at three venues in Ashland—two indoor stages (Angus Bowmer Theatre and the Thomas Theatre), and the intricately adorned flagship outdoor Allen Elizabethan Theatre, which opens in early June and runs through mid-October. Tickets to plays and special events (such as backstage tours) are available on the festival website, with a range of pricing that allows plenty of affordable options, as well as lots of seating choices. Many showings and events sell out in the weeks leading up to them, but OSF offers so many shows (up to five per day) that finding prime seating, even on short notice, is generally unproblematic.

In addition to the plays themselves, attendees can immerse themselves in a host of educational activities, including park talks, lectures, classes and workshops, and pre- and post-show conversations. Moreover, from June through October, the free evening Green Show offers an incredible lineup of talented performing artists representing many disciplines—dance, music, theater, martial arts, acrobatics, lectures, and more. The Green Shows are held six nights a week.

The theater experience at OSF is essentially casual and always convivial—a social scene on the bricks outside the theaters, along the city streets, in the lobby, and at the pre- and post-performance events. Attire is casual for most attendees, but dress warm for the outdoor theater and bring an extra layer for the air-conditioned indoor venues. At the plays, a few basic rules apply. Use of cameras or recording devices (including cell phones) is prohibited, and all shows begin promptly as scheduled, so there is no late seating. No outside food or beverages are allowed into the theaters, which have their own concessions, including local beers, wines, and ciders, which patrons 21 and over can enjoy in the lobby or in the theater seats. Children under the age of 6 are not allowed in the performances.

The culturally rich city of Ashland offers many diversions, both indoors and out: elegant and excellent high-end restaurants, diverse casual eateries and fun bars, numerous local wineries and several craft breweries, beautiful parks and many nearby hiking and biking trails, rafting plus world-class autumn fly fishing on the Rogue River, and many other options. Accommodations range from rustic to rarified, and OSF attendees should book lodging well in advance, especially during the busy summer season.

The OSF website offers everything needed to plan a visit, with copious information about every conceivable necessity and eventuality; further help is available through the always congenial Ashland Chamber of Commerce, www.ashlandchamber.com.

Oregon Shakespeare Festival stages plays from February through October in the thriving community of Ashland.

OREGON CHOCOLATE FESTIVAL

Ashland
Ashland Hills Hotel & Suites, 2525 Ashland Street
Early March
www.oregonchocolatefestival.com

The luxuriant scent of fine chocolate permeating the air in the Grand Ballroom at Ashland Hills Hotel testifies to the opulence of the Oregon Chocolate Festival held early each March to celebrate this delectable finery in all its splendid iterations. This popular three-day event features more than two dozen West Coast chocolatiers offering a mouthwatering assortment of chocolate edibles and ingenious chocolate-inspired creations, and also includes captivating and educational events.

The festival kicks off with at 5:30 pm on Friday with a social hour in the Stardust Lounge, where a small cover fee earns a chance to revel in appetizers and chocolate, including a chocolate fountain, while sipping a local wine or beer and conversing with festival chocolatiers to the accompaniment of live music. Next comes the spectacular, reservations-only Chocolate Makers Dinner at the historic Ashland Springs Hotel downtown in a charming and romantic ballroom, with seating beginning at 6:30. This semiformal affair features five incredible courses, each involving chocolate in incredibly sumptuous and creative nuances and paired with a local wine. This dinner sells out quickly, so reserve early via the Chocolate Festival website.

On Saturday, the festival kicks into high gear, delivering a full slate of intriguing demonstrations, classes, and vendors, as well as the spirited Chocolate Product Competition, in which chocolatiers enter their finest works to be judged by a panel of experts in hopes of earning one of the Best in Show categorical awards. Beyond the categorical

Preparing mouthwatering chocolate delectable at the Oregon Chocolate Festival.

awards, judges also select a coveted Best in Show award and attendees get in on the judging by selecting winners of the People's Choice awards.

Throughout the weekend, special classes and workshops at the Oregon Chocolate Festival, which require advance registration, allow participants the opportunity to learn unique skills and concepts under the tutelage of acknowledged experts. On Sunday morning, the popular and festive Charlie's Chocolate 5K Run/Walk and Kids' 400 Yard Dash start and end at the hotel, with participants encouraged to dress like their favorite characters from *Charlie and the Chocolate Factory*. Delicious prizes are served to all racers, including a Charlie's Chocolate Run Wonka Bar, as well as other take-home surprises.

The Oregon Chocolate Festival is a deservedly popular event in a community that boasts multitudinous activities; register early via the festival website and plan to stay for a while—the weekend and beyond, perhaps; take time to explore Ashland's diverse eateries, bars, pubs, parks, and attractions. Daily and two-day passes to the festival are modestly priced, and even the five-course Chocolate Maker's Wine Dinner is surprisingly affordable. Lodging options abound, including the festival venue itself.

OREGON CHEESE FESTIVAL

Central Point
Rogue Creamery, 311 N Front Street
Mid-March
www.oregoncheesefestival.com

Turophiles rejoice! The Oregon Cheese Festival is for you. Granted, *turophile* is an obscure word, but it means a lover of cheese, or connoisseur of cheese, and there's probably at least a little turophile in all of us, and nowhere better to sate your cheesy culinary desires than this increasingly popular, joyous celebration of all things cheese. The weekend-long Oregon Cheese Festival occupies two huge heated tents at Rogue Creamery in Central Point—15,000 square feet of cheese, cheese products, and cheese education, along with a variety of local and regional alcoholic beverages, local artisan foods, and more.

For a modest entry fee (at the door or in advance), attendees can sample a vast array of cow, goat, and sheep cheeses from Oregon creameries and watch a variety of demonstrations by creamery and culinary experts. The annual lineup is literally a who's who of Oregon cheese producers, ranging from the biggest creameries to the little-known outstanding boutique cheesemakers. An additional beverage fee (21 and over only) includes a collectible wine glass, etched with the Oregon Cheese Guild logo, for imbibing in craft ales, local wines, and ciders, and even try a variety of spirits produced right here in the Northwest. Kids and adults alike love the calves and kid goats on hand to showcase the beginnings of great milk producers, and the festival provides an array of other activities just for children. In recent years, nearly 5,000 people and some 100 vendors attend Oregon Cheese Festival, everyone reveling in the relaxed farmers'-market-style atmosphere.

Open from 11 am to 5 pm on Saturday and Sunday, the festival commences Friday night with the annual Meet the Cheesemakers Dinner featuring a special guest each year along with a host of Oregon cheesemakers. Proceeds from this special multicourse meal benefit the nonprofit Oregon Cheese Guild, founded in 2006 and dedicated to the art and craft of making cheese. The guild is a collaborative effort to increase awareness of Oregon's artisanal cheeses, create educational opportunities, and provide a platform for cooperation and shared resources among Oregon cheesemakers. Buy tickets to the dinner via the Cheese Festival website, but do so well in advance.

The host of Oregon Cheese Festival, USDA-certified organic Rogue Creamery, has operated since the 1930s, and its founder, Tom Vella, was both a visionary and a pioneer in the industry. He died at the age of 100 in 1998 and the business was inherited by his wife and four children. They eventually sold the business to the current owners who have continued in the spirit of the founding family.

Wine and cheese pairing at the Oregon Cheese Festival, held in beautiful Central Point.

ASHLAND WORLD MUSIC FESTIVAL

Ashland
Lithia Park, 150 Winburn Way
Late May
www.ashland.or.us/AWMF

Ashland's verdant Lithia Park is the idyllic scene for the Ashland World Music Festival, which hosts some of Southern Oregon's hottest musicians, from longstanding veterans in the Northwest music scene to the best up-and-coming artists. Each year, the festival selects musicians to cover a variety of multicultural genres—rock, reggae, soul, folk, blues, and more, including both traditional and contemporary sounds, along with a wide range of instrumental performers.

The Saturday festival runs from noon to 6 pm, with no admission fee, at the Butler Bandshell, a terrific venue for outdoor music, with groves of trees, often bubbling with singing birds in the mornings, shading a spacious manicured lawn that is ideal for setting up beach chairs or spreading a blanket. Chill out and enjoy the music or join the inevitable small crowd of fans dancing jubilantly in front of the stage. The relaxed vibe at this under-the-radar music fest is decidedly family friendly; locals spend the day enjoying the eclectic music and wonderful spring weather. A handful of food vendors are on hand, along with local art and craft vendors.

Lithia Park—an Ashland centerpiece—spans nearly 100 acres, stretching for a mile north to south, from downtown nearly to the Siskiyou National Forest boundary. In addition to the Bandshell, which hosts musical events throughout the summer, Lithia Park offers Japanese Gardens, two duck ponds, expansive undeveloped woodlands, a trail system, tennis and pickleball courts, a sand volleyball court, playground, ice rink (in winter), and picnic areas. The historic park was honored as one of the top ten Great American Spaces by the American Planning Association in 2014, and is the subject of *Lithia*

Ashland World Music Festival brings a laid-back vibe to verdant Lithia Park in Ashland.

Park: The Heart & Soul of Ashland (2016) by John Enders. The community of Ashland has a great deal more to offer visitors and the World Music Festival is a great event to highlight a long weekend spent exploring this beautiful city of 22,000 people.

BRITT MUSIC & ARTS FESTIVAL

Jacksonville
Britt Pavilion, 350 S 1st Street
Mid-June through mid-September
www.brittfest.org

Held throughout the summer in the historic 3,000-strong community of Jacksonville, about five miles west of Medford, the annual Britt Music & Arts Festival attracts thousands of enthusiasts to dozens of concerts representing myriad musical genres—classical, blues, jazz, folk, bluegrass, pop, country, and more. The performances are held outdoors in a naturally formed amphitheater set amid verdant forested hills at the estate of nineteenth-century photographer Peter Britt (1819–1905). With a maximum capacity of 2,200, the Britt Festival, a nonprofit endeavor dating back to the first small event in 1963, is able to attract world-class musicians while maintaining an intimate concert setting at each performance.

Concerts begin in the evening, typically under exquisitely clear Southern Oregon skies. Each year's concerts and ticket prices are announced by mid-April. Over the years, Britt has hosted some of the world's best-known acts—Chicago, Willie Nelson, Boz Scaggs, Diana Ross, Al Green, The B-52s, Randy Travis, and many more. But Britt also offers the chance to see up-and-coming stars, regionally known musicians, and veteran performers from every kind of music. Local restaurant concessions offer a wide array of great food, and both wine and beer are available onsite.

The summer-long Britt Music & Arts Festival stages an eclectic variety of outstanding music acts.

Britt does not sell tickets through third-party ticket agencies, either online or in person; tickets for all Britt performances are available through the event website, as well as at the festival box office at 216 West Main Street in Medford (open 9 am to 5 pm, Monday through Friday). The onsite Britt Hill box office is open on concert days from 3 pm through intermission, but for popular concerts, be sure to buy tickets well in advance. Attendees can buy reserved seating (stadium-style seating) or lawn space seating on the slope directly above the reserved section. Parking maps are available on the festival website and attendees need to consult these maps to avoid off-limits areas (most parking requires a bit of walking to reach the concert venue). Also plan for the summer heat: Jacksonville temperatures frequently hit the high nineties and even triple digits in high summer.

OREGON HONEY (& MEAD) FESTIVAL

Ashland
Ashland Elks Lodge, 255 E Main Street
Mid-August
www.oregonhoneyfestival.com

Celebrating honey in all its forms and uses as well as teaching people about pollinators and beekeeping and its many intricacies, the flavor-laden Oregon Honey Festival assembles an eclectic and interesting collection of speakers, environmentally oriented nonprofits, crafters, exhibitors, and vendors at the historic Ashland Elks Lodge for a full day of sampling and learning about everything from craft honey in countless iterations to mead and other beverages in which honey is a key ingredient.

Each year, a dozen or so beekeepers offer a wide range of honey for sampling and purchase. Other vendors specialize in gourmet cheese, chocolates, and other goodies, along with all the accoutrements of beekeeping such as beehives created from different types of wood. Backyard and small-scale beekeeping

Nectar Creek meads are among the wonderful Oregon products highlighted at the Oregon Honey (& Mead) Festival.

is an exciting way for families to develop an understanding of the natural environment and learn how to keep it healthy. Mead, an ancient, healthful fermented beverage, is a popular component of the event, with a who's who of Oregon producers sampling their delectable creations at the event.

The festival also includes a wide variety of educational activities, guest speakers, kids activities, live music, and more. Beekeeping associations have also participated, including experts from Klamath Basin Beekeepers Association, Southern Oregon Beekeepers Association, and Oregon State Beekeepers Association speaking on a variety of topics alongside authors, educators, and other bee and honey experts. Conservation is a critical component of the festival because some bee populations are in serious decline worldwide and many populations face a variety of environmental threats.

Tickets to the festival, available in advance (see festival website) and at the door, are modestly priced and include all the activities and events; children under 8 years old are admitted free. Downtown Ashland offers many great activities and eateries and the surrounding countryside is rich in opportunities for wine tasting, hiking, and other pursuits. Held during high summer, the Oregon Honey (& Mead) Festival is the perfect event to anchor a long weekend visiting Southern Oregon. Lodging options are numerous. The festival is hosted by Cascade Girl Organization, an educationally oriented, nonprofit organization supporting conservation and sustainable beekeeping practices, in cooperation with Ashland Parks and Recreation Department.

SUTHERLIN BLACKBERRY FESTIVAL

Sutherlin
Central Park and other venues
Third weekend in August
www.blackberry-festival.com

At first glance you may wonder where the blackberry fits into the Sutherlin Blackberry Festival, which seems to generate a lot more excitement for mud and vintage automobiles than berries: among the most popular events at this long-running, family-friendly summer festival are the uproarious mud volleyball tournament and the loud and sloppy mud truck races, along with the voluminous display of beautifully restored classic cars and trucks.

But blackberries make an appearance as well—not only do blackberry brambles grow profusely in the area, but the festival also invites chefs of all stripes to compete in the annual Blackberry Cook-Off. In the festival's earlier years, this culinary challenge had just a few categories, but now, contestants whip up scrumptious blackberry delights ranging from candies, confections, jams, and jellies to main course dishes, including ribs, kebabs, salmon, game hens, and more. Entry in the cook-off is open to anyone, with registration taking place Saturday morning. Judges are from all walks of life around the community—and many love their job so much that they return year after year to sample the delicacies.

Sutherlin's marquee festival begins with a cruise-in and poker run on Friday afternoon, followed by a street-party-style dance, with live music (see event website for locations). On Saturday, verdant Central Park hosts a full slate of activities, including the Blackberry Festival's huge car show, the Blackberry Cook-Off, mud volleyball, BMX races, four-wheel-drive barrel races, and lots of entertainment, along with numerous food and craft booths. Top the evening off with the classic car cruise and a dance in the streets of Sutherlin. The fun continues on Sunday with the motorcycle show, chili cook-off, diaper derby, and, of course, the mud races. Along with food, activities, and entertainment, the festival also features several drawings for fantastic prizes, including one lucky winner of a vintage automobile each year. The raffle monies go to good causes—not only to keep the event running but to provide

Vintage autos of all descriptions are a key part of the Sutherlin Blackberry Festival.

continuing education scholarships to graduates of Sutherlin and Oakland High Schools to help them in their quest to achieve a college education.

Now about that name, Blackberry Festival: in 1988, Wayne Calder, Bruce Long, and Donnie Moore met for lunch at Pat's Kozy Kitchen (a local's favorite and a hidden gem awaiting discovery by visitors) to discuss plans for a new community festival. One critical issue remained unresolved: what to name the event. The men were brainstorming as Pat Greer (owner of the diner) waited tables. Someone in the group said, "Well, blackberries are ripe this time of the year. Why don't we call it the Blackberry Festival?"

They all turned to Greer as if asking for approval. She agreed, saying, "Sounds good to me," and Blackberry Festival had its name. Long was the city manager at the time; Moore worked for a time in the city; and Calder was the chairman of the festival for its first twenty years. Greer became the festival secretary and has served in that capacity ever since. Pat's Kozy Kitchen opened in 1977 and epitomizes the affable, small-town charm of Sutherlin—a community of about 8,000 residents that readily welcomes visitors and offers an eclectic assortment of locally owned businesses and numerous avenues of outdoors recreation nearby.

BEAR CREEK SALMON FESTIVAL

Ashland
North Mountain Park, 620 N Mountain Avenue
First Saturday in October
www.bearcreeksalmonfestival.net

Salmon are integral to Pacific Northwest culture and have been for millennia; returning to their natal streams to spawn, the five species of Pacific salmon have historically been the engines that drove entire ecosystems, their staggering abundance barely imaginable by a modern society that bears witness to the many fragmentary populations of wild salmon that persist today in the watersheds of California, Oregon, and Washington. Southern Oregon's Rogue River watershed hosts annual runs of spring and fall chinook salmon and coho salmon (as well as steelhead).

The Bear Creek Salmon Festival not only celebrates salmon and wildlife habitat but also provides a fascinating educational experience. The setting on twenty-nine-mile-long Bear Creek in North Mountain Park is ideal because annually, fall chinook salmon return here to complete their life-cycles, spawning in the small stream to produce the next generation that will ultimately, as juveniles, migrate down Bear Creek and then down the Rogue River to reach the ocean; once there, they spend two to four years at sea, growing into the behemoths that will then return to Bear Creek.

Kids love the Salmon Story Tent at the Bear Creek Salmon Festival in Ashland.

The Bear Creek Salmon Festival (free admission) features all-ages interactive exhibits that focus on improving habitat for salmon and other species both at home and in the region. Participating exhibitors include federal, state, and local agencies, as well as a variety of conservation and activity-related organizations. Local experts provide details on a variety of related topics, such as water-conserving and pollinator-friendly gardening; Native American skills, such as traditional salmon cooking and basket making; fly fishing and fly tying; and of course lots of details about salmon and salmon habitat. Kids love the Salmon Story Tent and Salmon Spiral Labyrinth; and all ages are fascinated by the live bird of prey exhibit and talks by the members of Wildlife Images, a wildlife rehabilitation and education center located in nearby Grants Pass. The lineup of activities and exhibitors varies a bit from year to year (check the event website), but the enthusiasm and congeniality at this event never wavers. Throughout this one-day festival, local musicians provide entertainment and food is available from local vendors.

SOUTHERN OREGON SMOKED SALMON FEST

Medford
Pear Blossom Park, 312 E 4th Street
Late September to early October
www.southernoregonsmokedsalmonfest.com

Smoked salmon, a Northwest delicacy for centuries, is a diverse and complex culinary genre, far more so than most people realize. Recipes are legion, whether the fish in hand is ocean-caught coho or river-taken chinook, rich, dense sockeye from the famed runs British Columbia or pale meaty chum from the Yukon. In Southern Oregon, the famed Rogue River historically hosted massive runs of both chinook (king) and coho (silver) salmon, so Medford is the perfect place for the unique, family-friendly Southern Oregon Smoked Salmon Fest, which celebrates the mouthwatering sapidity of smoked salmon in myriad forms.

Attendees enjoy the opportunity to sample an array of smoked salmon offerings, while enjoying local and regional wines, beer, and other foods from the fertile Rogue Valley. A highlight of the festival is the smoked salmon competition, in which cash prizes are awarded to the winner as determined by a panel of judges composed of local restaurateurs, culinary experts, and community leaders. For a modest entry fee and advance registration, the contest is open to anyone. Festival attendees receive three voting tickets each with purchase of festival tickets. Throughout this one-day event, which runs from 1 pm to 5 pm at Medford's beautiful

Morsels of smoked chinook salmon await attendees at the Southern Oregon Smoked Salmon Fest.

Pear Blossom Park, live music entertains guests, and children enjoy carnival games and the park playground.

The Southern Oregon Smoked Salmon Fest not only celebrates an Oregon culinary mainstay, but also supports a fantastic cause: the event is the major public fundraiser for the Maslow Project, a nonprofit grassroots organization based in Medford that provides basic needs, crisis intervention, advocacy, street outreach, and essential support services to homeless children and their families in Southern Oregon. The project's overall mission is to offer every homeless child and youth the probability of success and the opportunity for a better life by providing resources for basic needs, removing barriers to education and employment, and fostering self-sufficiency in a collaborative and empowering environment. A key objective of this locally conceived organization is to help provide enough stability in the lives of children so that they can stay in school and complete their educations. For more information about the Maslow Project and other ways to provide essential financial support to the organization, visit www.maslowproject.com.

ASHLAND CULINARY FESTIVAL

Ashland
Ashland Hills Hotel & Suites, 2525 Ashland Street
    (event headquarters)
Early November
www.travelashland.org

One of the state's most amazing culinary events, the Ashland Culinary Festival offers four spectacular days of incredible cuisine, amazingly creative libations, and educational workshops, along with exuberant, entertaining, fast-paced cooking and mixology competitions, all celebrating Southern Oregon's diverse and eclectic food and drink and the people who bring them to life.

Home to many superb restaurants and bars, Ashland boasts a diversity of world-class chefs and imaginative victuallers, making the lively competitive events among the most popular aspects of the culinary festival. In the Chef Showdown, a dozen local chefs whip up their most ingenious and sumptuous offerings using local produce and a secret key ingredient revealed only at the start of the contest. Spurred on by a festival MC and a jubilant crowd, the chefs work their magic, and their creations are then judged by a panel of experts before the winner is decided. Additional contests ensue throughout the weekend, with the ever-popular Friday evening mixology competition and the Saturday Junior Chef Competition.

The festivities actually kick off on Thursday evening with the Ultimate Top Chef Dinner beginning at 6 pm at Ashland Hills Hotel & Suites, the event headquarters. This incredible multicourse dinner is prepared by all-star team composed of several of the amazingly talented Top Chef winners from years past, and each course is expertly paired with a local wine or ale. This exclusive, limited-seating dinner costs less than $100 per person, or tickets can be purchased as part of a four-day festival VIP package—but snag tickets as soon as they go on sale, as this popular gala event sells out quickly. Throughout the weekend, festival attendees can sample many different food specialties from regional restaurants, food artisans, and farms and sample wines and beers from some of the area's many wineries and breweries. Meanwhile, chefs and food specialists teach a variety of topics in limited-space hands-on workshops, with the intriguing lineup announced well ahead of the festival. Most workshops are limited to about two dozen participants to ensure a personal learning experience. Attendees must register for workshops when they buy festival tickets in advance (no seminar registration at the festival itself). Festival seminars are held at a variety of locations throughout Ashland.

Ashland Culinary Festival offers a variety of tickets and ticket packages: the VIP package includes the Top Chef Dinner as well as Friday's Culinary Kickoff, the Junior Chef Competition, Saturday and Sunday Chef Competitions and vendor sampling, one workshop per day (must preregister), and a commemorative wine glass and tasting punch card. The Three-Day Premier Package is identical but does not include the Top Chef Dinner. A variety of one-day and two-day ticket packages are also available, as are single-event tickets. For full details and to purchase tickets, which go on sale in September, visit the festival website.

Fresh produce awaits the celebrity chefs who compete at the Ashland Culinary Festival.

OREGON COAST FESTIVALS

OREGON COAST FESTIVALS

Oregon's incredibly scenic coastline stretches for nearly 400 miles, a mosaic of everything from rugged, wave-battered headlands to vast stretches of clean sand. US Highway 101 traces the Pacific shores from Astoria in the north to Brookings and the California border in the south, never venturing too far from the ocean and the myriad beaches, and spanning the numerous bays, rivers, and streams on historic bridges.

The Oregon coast has no large cities. Instead, Highway 101 and a few secondary roads thread through a string of wonderfully diverse small towns and tiny villages, some of them brimming with tourists much of the year and others largely off the radar. Astoria, Seaside, Cannon Beach, and Tillamook anchor the north coast, and each town differs markedly in character. On the central coast, Lincoln City, Newport, and Florence offer numerous attractions and amenities for visitors while smaller villages, such as Pacific City, Depot Bay, and Yachats, exude unique charm. The south coast—Coos and Curry Counties—are practically a world of its own. Coos Bay/North Bend is a sprawling port community, still very much a working town that has long been dependent on forestry and shipping; a short distance south, Bandon is somewhat the opposite—the classic touristy destination (with immediate access to gorgeous beaches).

But farther south still, into Curry County, Oregon's coastline reaches its scenic zenith, with small communities such as Gold Beach, Port Orford, and Brookings offering a palpable sense of discovery for visitors who seek their hidden-gem restaurants, pubs, shops, parks, and other attractions. The south coast beaches range from easily accessible and popular playgrounds to hidden enclaves reached by less-than-obvious trails that open up onto postcard-pretty expanses of unpeopled sand, and surf studded by rock spires (for a complete guide to all of Oregon's accessible beaches, see *Oregon Beaches, A Traveler's Companion* by John Shewey).

Oregon coast festivals come in many forms, celebrating all kinds of local activities and products. They include some of the state's oldest and most heavily attended events to festivals that remain virtually local secrets. Large and small, the coastal festivals are well worth attending and serve as excellent anchors for a long weekend spent exploring the Pacific shoreline.

GORSE BLOSSOM FESTIVAL

Bandon
Various venues
Mid-February
www.gorseblossomfest.com

The word *blossom* conjures images of lovely flowers, but there's nothing lovely about gorse (*Ulex europaeus*). It's a nasty invasive shrub, prickly and fast growing and able to outcompete native coastal shrubbery and form impenetrable thickets. This native of Europe is also inextricably bound, so it would appear, to the community of Bandon and its surrounds, for it was here, in the 1870s, that the town's founder, Lord George Bennett, first planted gorse. Sixty years later, gorse—resinous and highly flammable—was everywhere and then the unthinkable happened: a massive, fast-moving fire. Soon the town was aflame, the gorse being the prime fuel for the conflagration that gutted the community at the cost of ten lives and nearly 500 buildings.

To this day, gorse remains a major headache on the south coast, extremely difficult to control let alone eradicate. So why celebrate gorse? Is this a case of "if you can't beat it, join it"? Well, not exactly. The annual Gorse Blossom Festival is a celebration of the community and the environment, and in both realms, there is simply no escaping gorse in the Bandon area, so the event calls attention to the problem while treating festival goers to an incredibly good time. One of the festival founders, Todd Petrey, said, "It's the equivalent of seeing your aunt who is battling cancer wear a T-shirt that says, 'F*** Cancer.'" As such, one of the many popular activities at this wintertime party is tossing darts at a photo of Bennett, "the schmo who brought gorse here," as Petrey says.

The Gorse Blossom Festival is also a three-day culinary delight featuring special beermaker and winemaker dinners in which Oregon breweries and wineries team up with local restaurants, along with many different craft

If you can't beat it, well, celebrate it—sort of—at the Gorse Blossom Festival.

breweries, wineries, cideries, and distilleries joining a variety of excellent food purveyors in a sprawling vendor fair inside the Bandon Marketplace. Among the most popular activities at the festival are the Presidential Pub Crawl and the innovative Bloody Mary Hangover Stroll on Sunday morning: participants stroll through Old Town Bandon with their logo glasses and gather ingredients for their individualized Bloody Marys at stations every fifty yards or so, finally reaching the local distillery to add the critical touch, vodka. Tickets are limited in number, reasonably priced, and include both the glass and a T-shirt).

Bandon hosts a variety of other events as part of this three-day extravaganza, including the Oregon Coast Film Festival, and naturally festival attendees have ample opportunity to learn about that nasty gorse. A modest daily entry fee is required, and full weekend passes are available (visit the event website to buy tickets in advance, and for suggestions on lodging visit www.bandon.com). While in Bandon, be sure to visit the city's gorgeous beaches and check out the adjacent Bandon Marsh National Wildlife Refuge.

FESTIVAL OF DARK ARTS

Astoria
Fort George Brewery block, 1483 Duane Street
Mid-February
www.fortgeorgebrewery.com/festival-of-dark-arts

Don't be frightened by the name: while the Festival of Dark Arts brings together a bedazzling collection of unique artists and performers, from the brazen to the macabre, at its core this brew fest celebrates stout ales—the dark side of the brewer's craft, so to speak. It's a rather intimate setting—the city-block-size Fort George Brewery campus—with limited ticket sales (about 2,000 tickets), so sign up early via the Fort George Brewery website, and make hotel reservations early as well because Oregon's north coast really doesn't have an off season these days.

Annually the Festival of Dark Arts—the world's largest one-day stout fest—features some sixty stouts of all descriptions, including many limited-production ales, which attendees sample while being wowed by artists working in media such as ice, iron, and glass, and by dramatic performances by fire dancers, belly dancers, and much more. The event runs from noon to

10 pm, with live music throughout as well as food vendors, and the hours fly by all too quickly. Though specific details can change annually, in recent years all ticket holders received a Festival of Dark Arts Grimoire, a festival glass, and twelve drink tokens. Additional tokens are for sale at the festival.

Stout ales and the dark arts create a unique celebration at Fort George Brewery in Astoria.

Fort George Brewery, founded in 2007, annually invites a who's who of likeminded—or rather, dark-minded—regional brewers to the Festival of Dark Arts, even while offering more than a dozen of its own opaque ales for the celebration. The forty-odd breweries represented at Dark Arts brew up all kinds of intriguing concoctions, including ales aged in bourbon and wine barrels, every imaginable incarnation of traditional stouts, and innovative experimental brews using seemingly unlikely ingredients. During the light of a normal day, Fort George offers an impressive lineup of popular year-round beers and seasonal specialties, some of them distributed in cans, many others available only onsite. The Fort George Public House also boasts one of the best brewery food menus in the region.

NEWPORT SEAFOOD & WINE FESTIVAL

Newport
South Beach Marina, 2320 OSU Drive
Late February
www.seafoodandwine.com

Soon after its beginnings in 1977, the Newport Seafood & Wine Festival grew rapidly and within a few years ranked among the state's most heavily attended events of the kind. Held on the south side of Yaquina Bay in Newport, this popular event draws shoulder-to-shoulder crowds of enthusiastic patrons eager to try dozens upon dozens of state and regional wines and numerous culinary delights.

The festival occupies a massive tent at the Port of Newport in South Beach, adjacent to the Rogue Brewery facility, and the tent keeps the oft-tumultuous coastal winter weather at bay. The event offers a downloadable mobile-device app that provides all the latest details. Each year, the lineup of vendors—wineries, edibles, crafts—changes somewhat, but even four days amid the buoyant crowd would hardly be enough for any attendee to try more than a healthy sampling of the offerings. Many attendees happily stock up on wine at the festival, and both individual bottles and cases can be checked in and held at the coat/wine check for a nominal fee—a good idea because you can then continue to enjoy the festival unburdened by your liquid loot.

The festival begins Thursday at 5 pm and runs until 9 that evening (limited tickets available, online purchase only). Friday hours are noon to 9 pm, and Saturday hours are 10 am to 6 pm (online ticket sales only for Saturday); Sunday hours are 10 am to 4 pm. Note that the Newport Seafood & Wine Festival is a 21-and-over event—children and people under 21 years of age are not allowed. Wine and food samples cost a small fee (staring at $1), and full glass pours and full-meal servings are also available. Most vendors at the festival accept debit and credit cards, although the WiFi connection to process cards can get slow during peak hours, and the venue has two onsite ATM machines (the event WiFi is a free network with no password).

The festival venue, as well as the nearby Oregon Coast Aquarium, both have spacious parking lots (with a small fee required to park for the festival),

Newport Seafood & Wine Festival has been going strong for more than 40 years.

and several public lots are located nearby, but all tend to fill completely during the event. However, the Newport Seafood & Wine Festival provides a free bus shuttle to and from the event, with stops at many of the local hotels, motels, and popular Newport neighborhoods. Shuttles stop running one hour after the closing of the festival. On Saturday the hours are extended for service to area restaurants.

Also, a number of licensed temporary cab services, along with regular Newport cab services, can provide transportation. Expect a line to get in (it moves along quickly), so plan accordingly. Notably, the hotels on the south side of the bay, within walking distance of the festival, book up completely, so securing a room at one of them requires reservation well in advance.

SAVOR CANNON BEACH WINE & CULINARY FESTIVAL

Cannon Beach
Various venues
Mid-March
www.savorcannonbeach.com

One of the most popular destination communities on the entire Pacific Northwest coast, beautiful Cannon Beach stretches along a gorgeous strip of clean, white sand, with iconic Haystack Rock sitting just offshore, creating a postcard pretty panorama. The town boasts excellent restaurants, lively bars, wine shops, breweries, art galleries, clothiers, and myriad shops of all descriptions.

Cannon Beach also hosts one of the best wine and culinary festivals in Oregon. Savor Cannon Beach Wine & Culinary Festival is a four-day celebration of Northwest-centric wine, cuisine, and arts. A series of festival events focus on specific themes that showcase the bounty of Northwest wine and cuisine, while the town's restaurants, galleries, and shops feature a weekend full of tastings, special dinners, and cultural events. Most of the wine tasting events are intimate, though the largest event of the festival, the Saturday Wine Walk, accommodates several hundred wine tasters who can visit approximately forty Northwest wineries pouring tastings at Cannon Beach art galleries, restaurants, and retail shops, all within easy walking distance in this compact beach community.

Other festival wine tasting events—which tend to vary from year to year—showcase award-winning or notable wines from the Pacific Northwest. The festival kicks off on Thursday with Best of the Northwest, a wine tasting throw-down in which participants taste twelve selected wines representing different wine-growing regions of Oregon and Washington, then vote on their favorites to determine the evening's top wines. Friday's events typically include Winemaker's Premium Pours, in which a number of Northwest wineries each pour three special wines that may include library wines, verticals, horizontals, or reserve selections. For wine enthusiasts who want to improve their wine aptitude, a Saturday seminar, Taste Like an Expert, serves several wines and focuses on wine tasting skills, terminology and etiquette. On Sunday, participants can indulge

Haystack Rock provides a scenic backdrop for events at Cannon Beach.

in Gold Medal Wines & Battle of the Bites, featuring twelve Gold Medal wines from the SavorNW Wine Awards and "bites" offered by area chefs and restaurants. Participant votes determine which bite wins the battle.

Again, though, Savor Cannon Beach likes to keeps things fresh, typically altering the event lineup each year—so buy tickets and come discovery the fun. Tickets (purchase through the festival website) are available for individual events, or you can buy a full festival pass good for admission to all festival tasting events. Advance purchase is recommended as events are limited in size and often sell out.

POURING AT THE COAST

Seaside
Seaside Civic and Convention Center, 415 1st Avenue
Mid-March
www.pouringatthecoast.com

With its title an effective play on words considering the oft-wet weather on the Oregon coast in March, Pouring at the Coast is billed as the "perfect pairing of brew and beach." That claim might be arguable, considering how well a regional microbrew pairs with the beach on a sunny summer day, but this craft beer celebration has rapidly gained momentum as one of the north coast's most fun and relaxed brew festivals.

Pouring at the Coast still remains a bit under the radar, like a secret you've discovered that you can't wait to share with just a few close friends, and the perfect sojourn for ale aficionados who enjoy seeking the state's

quieter and less commercialized beer festivals. Pouring at the Coast annually attracts as many as thirty local and regional breweries pouring dozens of ales. A central stage features ongoing live music; numerous large tables allow attendees to sit down, relax with a beer, and chat with fellow microbrew fans; food vendors serve a variety of local fare. A

Embrace the winter rains at the Oregon Coast... and then head inside to sample regional ales at Pouring at the Coast.

modest two-tiered entry fee (three beer tickets or ten beer tickets) includes a souvenir glass, and additional beer tickets are available for a few dollars each.

The event typically begins in midafternoon and ends around 8 pm. As the ales flow downstairs during the festival, a homebrew competition rages upstairs, with winners announced at the end of the show; the rules are posted on the event website. Finally, Pouring at the Coast bestows a People's Choice award to the favorite beer at the event as voted on by attendees; thus far, two Northwest standouts—GoodLife Brewing (Bend) and Wild Ride Brewing (Redmond)—have each earned first-place honors twice.

Although Seaside can be a busy and bustling tourist destination—and why not, considering its big, broad, beautiful sand beach and the wonderful boardwalk running alongside it, not to mention many fine eateries and interesting shops—parking is usually unproblematic. Adjacent to the convention center, a large free public lot easily accommodates the Pouring at the Coast crowd. Street-side parking is likewise abundant.

BIRDING & BLUES FESTIVAL

Pacific City
Kiawanda Community Center,
    34600 Cape Kiwanda Drive (event headquarters)
Late April
www.birdingandblues.org

In a unique fusion, this annual award-wining event celebrates a favorite coastal activity—birdwatching—with an evening accompaniment of blues music over the course of three days during the height of spring migration for myriad species of birds that annually stop along Oregon's estuaries, beaches, and nearshore waters. The Birding & Blues Festival features expert speakers presenting on a variety of bird-related topics as well as field trips to local birding hotspots (including kayak tours and dory boat outings). Seminars and presentations are held at the Kiawanda Community Center on Cape Kiwanda Drive on the west side of the Nestucca River.

Nearby, Cape Kiwanda Beach and its namesake headland, and the picturesque offshore sea stack—Haystack Rock—comprise the most popular shoreline in the area for visitors (ever-popular Pelican Brewing Company sits beside the large parking lot serving the beach). Friday and Saturday evenings after the birding activities, festival attendees are treated to live acts performed by notable bands and musicians from throughout the region. Attendees can choose from a variety of registration-fee options. A modestly priced deluxe pass (see event website) provides access to all presentations, field trips, and concerts.

Local birdwatching venues are both numerous and productive for a variety of species. Nestucca Bay is a narrow estuary gathering both the Nestucca and Little Nestucca Rivers and is a hotspot for waterfowl, shorebirds, wading birds, and raptors. Nestucca Spit separates the lower river from the ocean and is preserved as Bob Straud State Park; both the west (ocean) side and east (river) side of the two-mile-long peninsula are prime locations for spring birdwatching and accessible by trails and beach walking. One of Oregon's newest state parks, Sitka Sedge State Natural Area, just north of Tierra Del Mar and about 3.5 miles north of Cape Kiwanda, encompasses nearly 400 acres of the Sand Lake Estuary (with some 5 miles of hiking trails), and complements Clay Myers State Natural Area on Whalen Island just to the north. These areas provide public access to some of the best birdwatching on the central coast and festival field trips visit these and other hotspots.

Kaleidoscopic Harlequin Ducks are among the many species birders might see during the Birding & Blues Festival.

ASTORIA WARRENTON CRAB, SEAFOOD & WINE FESTIVAL

Astoria
Clatsop County Fair & Expo Center,
  92937 Walluski Loop
Last full weekend in April
www.astoriacrabfest.com

Anywhere else, you'd raise eyebrows by wearing a bright-red crab hat—a beanie with big black googly eyes and dangling red legs and pincers. But at one of Oregon's most beloved and popular coastal events, such attire is ubiquitous. The annual Astoria Warrenton Crab, Seafood & Wine festival launched as a humble little celebration of Dungeness crab—one of the state's signature seafood products—in 1982. Nearly four decades later, this multi-award-winning extravaganza has outgrown several venues in Astoria and Warrenton, and now attracts about 15,000 people per year, along with nearly 200 vendors offering everything from incredible cuisine to trend-setting art—among them are more than fifty regional (mostly Oregon) wineries and a few local breweries. A central theme, of course, is a celebration and appreciation of Oregon seafood and Oregon wine, but this event has grown to a joyous three-day party, with live music entertaining attendees from two different stages throughout the festival.

The festival begins Friday at 4 pm, closes at 9 that night, and then ramps up again at 10 am Saturday, running until 8 pm. Sunday hours are 11 to 4. Parking at the event site—the Clatsop County Fair & Expo Center—is a bit limited and fills to capacity at prime times during the festival, particularly Saturday. Significantly, the expo center does not have parking for RVs or trailers. Fortunately the Astoria–Warrenton Chamber of Commerce (www.oldoregon.com) arranges a shuttle-bus service for the festival and the city has a variety of public park-and-ride locations. Shuttle bus service is limited on Sunday, running only from the Port of Astoria Public Park & Ride at Pier 2. The shuttle costs a small fee per person, round trip (cash only with no change

Delectable Dungeness crab is the star at the Astoria Warrenton Crab, Seafood & Wine Festival.

given). Latest transportation details are always posted on the festival website. Lodging in the area fills up for the weekend, so book early (consult the chamber of commerce for options).

So many wineries compose a central attraction of the event that a wine competition is a natural: each year, the participating wineries are invited to enter wines in the festival's wine competition. A panel of judges samples and scores each wine during a blind tasting, with the top-scoring red wines and white wines then tasted again by the judges. The winning red and white wines are awarded the title of Best of Show. Additional top-scoring wines are awarded gold, silver, and bronze medals. Moreover, the general public enjoys a fun opportunity to participate in the pre-festival UnWined, a small event directly following the blind tasting competition in early March. Ticket holders to UnWined get to sample the wines and vote for the People's Choice award. Best of Show, medal-winning, and the People's Choice award wines are listed on the festival website. The UnWined event is held at Astoria's Liberty Theater (see the festival website for tickets and information).

NEWPORT PAPER & BOOK ARTS FESTIVAL

Newport
Newport Visual Arts Center and other venues
Third weekend in April
www.coastarts.org/about/programs/
    newport-paper-arts-festival/

Launched in 1994, the Newport Paper & Book Arts Festival is the only paper festival of its kind on the Oregon coast and the largest of its kind on all the West Coast; it draws attendees from the greater Northwest and beyond. The annual festival features three days of innovative, informative, and exciting one-day workshops celebrating papermaking, surface embellishment, bookmaking, bindings, articles made of paper, and techniques and tools for working with paper and fibers. The festival is organized by the Oregon Coast Council for the Arts and held at several venues around town, including the Newport Visual Arts Center in the trendy and captivating Nye Beach District west of Highway 101.

Each year for three days, the festival gathers award-winning art instructors who are leaders in their specific disciplines to teach workshops on a wide array of art media. These workshops include new and innovative techniques as well as traditional processes. Previous workshops have included Asian, Coptic, and Japanese bookbinding, miniature books, papermaking, paper casting, silk paper, paste papers, paper jewelry, suminigashi (paper marbling), orizomegami and itajime (folded paper resist dyeing), paper basketry, Japanese surface design techniques, greeting cards with book structures,

Newport Paper & Book Arts Festival spotlights the amazing talents of paper artists from around the region.

box construction, paper lamps and screens, stamp art, woodblock, linoleum and Safety-Kut printing, collage, and mixed-media embellishments.

Workshops last up to six hours, beginning at 9:30 am and ending by 4:30 pm, with a one-hour lunch break; classrooms can accommodate from eight to sixteen students, with each class size determined by the instructor, as well as room size and availability of services. To make sure attendees from the Northwest and beyond all have equal opportunity to sign up for classes, initial registration is accepted by postmark date, with the festival brochure mailed out in late January each year (it includes all pricing information). Registrations are not accepted by email or over the phone. If you are interested in attending the festival and are not currently on the brochure mailing list, email the registrar at npaf@coastarts.org or call (541) 265-6540 to be added.

LAKESIDE CRAWDAD FESTIVAL

Lakeside
Tenmile Lake County Park
Mother's Day weekend in early May
www.facebook.com/Lakeside-Crawdad-Festival-321710537538/

Lots and lots of boiled crawfish, loads of cooked shrimp, maybe some alligator sausage; throw in some pirates and their wenches, and all kinds of great live music—yes, Lakeside is a bit of a drive for most Oregonians, but the annual Lakeside Crawdad Festival is a frolicking good time that makes the perfect capstone for a Mother's Day weekend spent on the south coast.

Aptly named Lakeside, the close-knit community on the shores of sprawling, sinuous Tenmile and North Tenmile Lakes, about equidistant between Reedsport and North Bend, throws out the welcome mat for one of only two festivals in the state dedicated to the crayfish—aka crawdad—a freshwater shellfish especially popular in Southern cuisine. Annually the Lakeside Crawdad Festival burns through, or rather boils through, some 300 pounds of crawfish shipped in from Louisiana, the heartland of Cajun and Creole cooking, and anyone who waits until Sunday midday risks sadly discovering that the fest has run out of this scrumptious delicacy. Alongside

Lakeside Crawdad Festival remains a pleasantly quaint community festival.

the crawdad tails and claws, shrimp and alligator are on the menu. Bring an appetite because crawdad and shrimp are available in both half-pound and full one-pound meals, and alligator is available in both two-piece and three-piece meals as well as on a stick. Samplers are available for anyone who has never tried these three delicacies. Prices are very reasonable and you can wash down these rare treats with a beer or wine in the beer garden.

Throughout the three-day event, some of the region's top musicians entertain the ebullient crowds, and a variety of vendors offers arts, crafts, foods, and others wares at the extensive street fair running alongside the crawfish festivities. Friday evening, the fun kicks off with a crawdad-eating contest, and throughout the weekend chefs compete in cooking contests, while kids get to catch live crawfish for the crawdad races and revel in the kids carnival.

Since its inception in 2007, the Lakeside Crawdad Festival has continued to gain attention throughout the state—to the tune of more than 10,000 attendees by its second year. So leave nothing to chance: book lodging or reserve a nearby campsite well in advance and make a weekend of it.

FLORENCE RHODODENDRON FESTIVAL

Florence
Florence Events Center, 715 Quince Street
Third weekend in May
www.florencechamber.com/annual-events/rhody-festival/

Launched in 1908, the same year as the inaugural Portland Rose Festival, the Florence Rhododendron Festival is the oldest floral festival in Oregon, and the second oldest on the West Coast. Each year, this multifaceted citywide celebration draws throngs of visitors to this otherwise quiet and charming central-coast community of nearly 9,000 residents. Laura Johnson reigned as the first festival queen and decades later explained that key local citizens started the event to draw tourists and their dollars to the town, and the peak of the rhododendron bloom seemed the ideal time—the showy shrubs abound in the coastal woodlands. That first year, the widely known itinerant frontiersman and poet Joaquin Miller, uncle of Johnson's future husband, Melvin Miller, was chosen as Grand Marshall, a shrewd ploy to lend credibility to the event.

Since those early years, the Rhododendron Festival has grown into one of the coast's most anticipated annual festivals, each year sporting a different theme. People come from all over the state and beyond, transforming Florence into a lively, bustling, vibrant little city that rolls out the welcome mat for all the visitors and treats them to a host of interesting and entertaining events and activities. Throughout the weekend, one of the big draws is the spectacular rhododendron display in which hundreds of the beautiful flowers garnish the Florence Events Center. The festival officially begins with the Thursday night Rhododendron Court coronation, and the crowning of the year's Queen Rhododendra and King of the Coast, naturally held amid the blossoms at the Event Center. On Friday, the festival's carnival proves a big hit with kids (and lasts late into the night for older kids), continuing through the weekend; the annual arts festival sponsored by the Florence Regional Arts Alliance begins at the Events Center and continues through the weekend. At the local Three Rivers Casino Resort, the Let it Ride vendor fair begins on Friday, and through the weekend, the casino hosts a variety of Let it Ride events focused on the motorcycle culture that has become a big part of the Florence Rhododendron Festival.

On Saturday morning, runners converge at the Events Center for the Rhody Run, which has been part of the festival for more than forty years, and the Maple Street Vendor Fair takes over Old Town from 10 am until 6 pm. At the casino, Saturday brings the Let it Ride Motorcycle Show, and not to be outdone by the two-wheelers, the Beachkomer's Car Club sponsors a popular, colorful Show 'n' Shine featuring beautifully

Blooming Rhododendrons in the verdant coastal forest near Florence

restored vintage automobiles. The Rhody Festival Junior Parade is a huge draw on Sunday. Throughout the festival, many other events, varying somewhat annually, make this vibrant coastal community a great place to visit.

In addition to the Rhododendron Festival and its myriad activities, Florence—Oregon's Coastal Playground, as the local chamber accurately proclaims—offers ready access to outstanding sand beaches and coastal recreation activities. Florence boasts a variety of excellent restaurants, along with numerous lodging options (book well in advance for Rhody Fest weekend).

ROCKAWAY BEACH KITE FESTIVAL

Rockaway Beach
Rockaway Beach Wayside
Late May
www.rockawaybeach.net/events/kite-festival/

One of the longest-running kite festivals in the Northwest, the Rockaway Beach Kite Festival launched—so to speak—way back in 1977 at this alluring little oceanfront town strategically located about midway between hyper-popular Cannon Beach to the north and the richly interesting Tillamook area to the south. The kite fest is sponsored by the American Kitefliers Association (AKA), an international organization that is the largest association of kite fliers and kite clubs in the world. The AKA is actively involved in a variety of other Oregon kite festivals, and the beach events are always a big hit—what better place to enjoy colorful kites and gorgeous scenery?

The Rockaway Beach Kite Festival transforms the lovely sand beach

here into an aerial kaleidoscope of vibrant colors and patterns. The event includes friendly unofficial competitions, and contestants can win awards not only for the nicest kite, but also for some fun categories, such as the kite that drags on the ground the longest before becoming airborne. The festival

Colorful kites fill the skies at Rockaway Beach during the town's annual Kite Festival.

features special classes for kids, teaching them how to build and fly their own small kites, as well as a variety of demonstrations and exhibitions by veteran kite flyers. Kite enthusiasts are also encouraged to bring their own kites to fly.

Throughout the long weekend, the festival also provides outstanding live music by regional artists, along with a variety of vendors that include kite paraphernalia, craftspeople, and great food choices. In addition to the festival activities on the beach and at the spacious wayside, Rockaway Beach offers a variety of tantalizing restaurants, interesting shops, and outstanding beaches. Access to the area beaches is excellent—from the mouth of the Nehalem River at the north end of town (Nedonna Beach) to the scenic Twin Rocks Beach at the south end of town. The community provides numerous beach-access sites, most of them unmarked at the west terminus of the side streets off Highway 101.

BROOKINGS AZALEA FESTIVAL

Brookings
Various venues
Memorial Day weekend
www.brookingsharborchamber.com

In 1939, the state of Oregon opted to dedicate a new state park at the outskirts of the then-tiny community of Brookings. The site was chosen because of its prodigious and beautiful native western azaleas (*Rhododendron occidentale*).

The Azalea Parade is one of many events included in the Brookings Azalea Festival.

WL Crissey and Elmer Bankus, well-known local citizens and members of the Brookings Chamber of Commerce, felt the dedication ceremony for Azalea State Park should be a showy, extravagant affair, and conceived the Azalea Festival. The inaugural event, with state parks superintendent Samuel H. Boardman in attendance and the azaleas in full bloom, was a regal success, with a variety of events, including a parade, Azalea Queen coronation, and a nightcap banquet featuring barbequed hog. That evening amid the fanfare, according to state parks historian WA Langille, the locals decided the event should continue annually. World War II, however, intervened, and after the even larger festivals of 1940 and 1941, the event was suspended as the nation had more pressing matters weighing on its collective conscious. After the war, the festival began anew and continued to expand in scope and attendance.

Today, this sprawling, multiday festival draws some 15,000 attendees annually and features a wide variety of activities and events held throughout Brookings-Harbor. Hundreds of participants make the Azalea Parade on Saturday a key part of the celebration, with spectators lining the route, and an expansive street fair features many dozens of vendors. The event continues the tradition of crowning an Azalea Queen from a court of princesses, and the park itself is headquarters for several key events, including the presentation of the queen as well as the festival grand marshall and the Pioneer Citizens. Associated events during the five-day-long community-wide celebration include a classic car show, quilt show, carnival, book sale, veterans events, and the prodigious Azalea Festival Art Show, which draws some 150 exhibitors.

At the two-day art show (free admission), local and regional artists, from novices to professionals, display and sell their works, and skilled artists conduct workshops throughout the show. Out-of-town judges select winning entries in the art competition, and special awards are chosen by the Azalea Festival Queen, Grand Marshall of the Parade, and the Pioneer Citizens. All show visitors may vote for the People's Choice award. Meanwhile, down in the adjoined town of Harbor, local Chetco Brewing Company sponsors Rock the Chetco, a lively, festive, weekend-long party featuring craft beers, great food, games, brewing competition, artisan market, and outstanding live music.

More than two dozen different events, activities, and associated celebrations make up the Brookings Azalea Festival, with the schedule posted on the fest website well in advance. Because Azalea Fest is held over Memorial Day weekend and attracts lots of visitors, be sure to reserve lodging well in advance.

LAKESIDE BREWFEST

Lakeside
Wulfy Beach, Tenmile Lake County Park
Father's Day weekend in mid-June
www.facebook.com/lakesidebrewfest/

Location, location, location. And for a brew fest, it doesn't get much better than a summer day at the beautiful new Wulfy Beach on Tenmile Lake. Hosted by the city of Lakeside, a friendly little waterside community that annually draws boaters and RVers by the throngs to play at Tenmile Lake and the nearby beaches, the Lakeside Brewfest features most of Oregon's south coast breweries, as well as a few surprise vendors from afar. In recent years, even a few craft cider producers and wineries have joined the fray.

Beginning on Friday afternoon and running through Saturday, the festival features live music, as well as a variety of ancillary activities for both adults and children. The festival vendors set up under canopy tents on the extensive lawn at Wulfy Park; the park features dozens of palm trees and an extensive sand beach, not to mention a commanding view of Tenmile Lake and the surrounding evergreen-cloaked coastal hills. Tenmile Lake County Park sits adjacent to Wulfy Park and features a large public boat ramp. Visitors can literally boat in to the brew fest, with larger boats using the county park's

Sunshine prevails at the Lakeside Brewfest at Tenmile Lake.

mooring and small craft such as kayaks paddling right up to the beach.

The brew fest makes a great primary destination, as does Tenmile Lake—the lake itself, with Lakeside as the hub, offers superb water skiing and other water sports, and is one of Southern Oregon's best fisheries for largemouth bass, panfish, and large yellow perch. Lakeside is just ten miles north of Coos Bay and offers all basic services and amenities—including a handful of fun restaurants, including Up the Creek Tavern on 8th Street, just a five-minute walk from the brew fest, as well as the restaurant at Lakeside Shore Lodge, which has window seats overlooking the Tenmile Lake. Entry fees for the brew fest are nominal and include the logo-inscribed tasting glass.

ASTORIA SCANDINAVIAN MIDSUMMER FESTIVAL

Explore Astoria
Discover your inner Viking!

Astoria Scandinavian
Midsummer Festival

Astoria
Clatsop County Fairgrounds, 92937 Walluski Loop
Third full weekend in June
www.astoriascanfest.com

The Pacific Northwest enjoys a rich Nordic heritage, having attracted immigrants from Scandinavia (Denmark, Norway, and Sweden) and Finland as early as the mid-1800s, and in just a twenty-year period, from 1890 to 1910, more than 150,000 Scandinavians settled in the Pacific Northwest. Astoria, the first permanent US settlement on the Pacific Coast and incorporated as a city in 1876, attracted Scandinavian and Finnish settlers in substantial numbers in the late nineteenth century, many of them migrating there to earn a living fishing the bountiful Columbia River. To this day, many descendants of the Nordic immigrants still reside in and around Astoria.

This pleasant and popular north coast community celebrates its Nordic roots each year with the Astoria Scandinavian Midsummer Festival. Historically midsummer was celebrated on the feast day of Saint John the Baptist, but its roots can be traced to pre-Christian solstice celebrations; in 1952, the Swedish Parliament decreed that this major festival be held on a weekend, so it always falls between June 20 and 26. The Midsummer Festival in Astoria began its modern incarnation as a Brownie troop presentation in 1968, and soon grew into a citywide celebration. During its three-day run, this colorful and educational event features myriad Scandinavian musical, dance, and theater group performances, as a well as an engaging array of traditional Midsummer Fest activities, and numerous vendors offering handcrafts, imported Scandinavian goods, and traditional Scandinavian foods. Special meals—Beef Dinner, Viking Dinner, Midnight Sun Breakfast, Pannukakku Breakfast—provide a chance to try traditional preparations at very modest prices.

The vendor area and beer gardens open on Friday afternoon, and Friday evening brings the Queen's Coronation in which a panel of judges selects Miss Scandinavia for that year. This festive event includes presentations on Scandinavian heritage as well as theatrical performances, and then ushers in the Torchlight Parade, in which Scandia men bearing flaming torches escort the newly crowned Miss Scandinavia and audience members to the bonfire to throw straw hexes into the flames. This tradition symbolizes ridding oneself of bad luck for the year. Accordionists play tunes and dances tend to break out around the fire. Saturday kicks off with the Midnight Sun Breakfast and the Running of the Trolls (register online or at the festival), with several footrace distances to choose from. Entertainment, ongoing throughout the weekend, highlights superb musicians and actors, and also includes a living history display called the Empire of Chivalry and Steel Viking Encampment, in which costumed reenactors demonstrate crafts, tournaments, armor making, and combat arts from the culture of the Middle Ages.

The festival parade begins midday on Saturday, featuring Miss Scandinavia and her court, costumed dancers and entertainers, representatives from the Scandinavian lodges, and family groups parading through the arena and festival grounds to the outdoor stage for the traditional Flag Raising and Midsummer Pole ceremony. Saturday festivities go deep into the night, with a variety of additional activities held throughout the day and evening, including the Parade

Celebrate Nordic heritage at the Astoria Scandinavian Midsummer Festival.

of Costumes, providing attendees a chance to speak with traditionally attired festival participants about their costumes. Hungry fest-goers can dive into traditional foods of many kinds, with lefse (Norwegian flat bread) being a major attraction. Ultimately the Astoria Scandinavian Midsummer Festival comes to a close with a formal flag ceremony on Sunday afternoon, but not before throngs of attendees have garnered newfound appreciation for the Northwest's Nordic heritage and perhaps their own family histories.

CLAMBOREE & GLASS ART FESTIVAL

Coos Bay
Empire District, various venues
Late June
coosbay.org/clamboree-and-glass-art-fest

What do bivalves and blown-glass art have in common? Simple: they share the spotlight at one the south coast's most joyous and intriguing community festivals, the Clamboree & Glass Art Festival, held each summer in Coos Bay's historic Empire District. Founded as Empire City in 1853, the town ultimately voted to become part of Coos Bay in 1965. The district occupies the bayfront on the west edge of the city, once a thriving working waterfront. The entirety of the Coos Bay estuary system has long been famous for excellent clamming prospects, so much so that to this day the gaper clam is locally called an Empire clam.

Fittingly, clams are a big part of Clamboree, served up in a variety of delectable forms by food vendors—clam chowder, grilled clams, clam hoagies, and even clam cakes. Many other wonderful foods are available, and adults

Kids love the tractor train at the Clamboree & Glass Art Festival.

21 and over can partake in local craft ales from 7 Devils Brewing or choose wine or even spirits. Meanwhile, the festival's other top-billed attraction, the glass blowers, demonstrate and sell their intricate and beautiful creations, while an eclectic lineup of live music entertains fest-goers throughout the day. In addition to live music, Clamboree always serves up new entertainment surprises, which over the years have included folk dancers, a drum group, a magician, hula dancers and ukulele players, and old-time fiddlers.

Moreover, one of the most popular events at this congenial festival is a one-of-a-kind in Oregon, the annual Hollerin' Contest, held at the aptly named Hollering Place Wayside. In this case, the Hollerin' Contest is intricately tied to local history: Coos Bay is a narrow inlet, about a half mile across from Empire to the North Spit. The actual Hollering Place is across the bay from the wayside; Native Americans would stand on the north side of the bay and holler across the channel for a ride to the other side. Someone from the village would then canoe across to get them. When white settlers arrived, they adopted the same custom. Today this tradition carries on in the jovial Hollerin' Contest, in which contestants belt out as many decibels as they can muster, with their lungpower measured with a meter. The most boisterous contestants in each of three categories—men, women, and kids—win prizes donated by local merchants.

Clamboree stretches for several blocks, and along the way are a host of other activities, including open houses with demonstrations, interpretive displays, and sales at the Coos Bay Boat Building Center, the beautiful historic Tower House (built in 1872 and now a B&B), and the Confederated Tribes of Coos, Lower Umpqua and Siuslaw Tribal Hall. There is no admission fee; just show up on Saturday morning, park at one of lots at or near the waterfront, and spend the day in revelry.

LINCOLN CITY SUMMER KITE FESTIVAL AND FALL KITE FESTIVAL

Lincoln City
D River State Recreation Site
Late June and early fall
www.oregoncoast.org/lincoln-city-summer-kite-festival
www.oregoncoast.org/lincoln-city-fall-kite-festival

Lincoln City's beautiful D River Beach comes alive with color during the Kite Festival.

Lincoln City throws two popular Saturday/Sunday kite festivals each year, one in late June (Lincoln City Summer Kite Festival) and one in early fall (Lincoln City Fall Kite Festival), both held at the beautiful sand beach in the center of town at D River Wayside. These kaleidoscopic celebrations feature incredible displays of kite flying with massive, eye-popping kites of all descriptions handled by experts.

From simple handmade diamond-shaped kites like those we all flew as kids to the most elaborate novelty kites, every style of kite is represented at these family-friendly festivals, and at peak times the vibrant-blue summer sky over the beach literally swarms with incredible kites of all descriptions. In addition to the super-popular and colorful "big kites," expert flyers also demonstrate stunt kites and other specialty styles. Events include the festive Running of the Bols, in which participants do their best to run the beach into the wind to launch and fly big, circular, spinning, bol-style kites, the Kids Kite Parade on the Beach, and the free kite-making workshops for kids. The daily schedule can vary based on weather conditions, but the beach and the surrounding area is well worth exploring no matter the weather.

The spectacular kite displays and the fun festival activities make the Lincoln City Kite Festivals must-see spectacles, and this central-coast community offers many other activities and attractions: quiet stretches of beach with little-known hidden access points, fantastic shops of every description, eateries ranging from great seafood restaurants to regionally renowned dinner houses, a popular craft brewery, countless lodging options, crabbing and fishing on Siletz Bay, and much more. Though spacious, the parking lot at D River Wayside fills up on festival weekends, so arrive early. Otherwise park at the nearby Lincoln City Community Center or Lincoln City Outlets and use the free shuttle, which runs continuously from 10 am to 4 pm both Saturday and Sunday. D River Wayside is within easy walking distance of a variety of restaurants, lodging options, and shops, as well as pleasant D River State Recreation Site.

SOUTHERN OREGON KITE FESTIVAL

Brookings
Port of Brookings-Harbor Kite Field
Third weekend in July
www.southernoregonkitefestival.com

Anchoring Oregon's south coast, the community of Brookings offers everything a traveler could want—incredible beaches, myriad lodging options, fun restaurants, intriguing shops, wonderful weather much of the time, and a variety of enjoyable annual events, including one of the premier kite festivals in the United States. Since 1993, the Southern Oregon Kite Festival has attracted some of the best-known kite fliers and kite makers, all there to perform with bedazzling kites of all kinds and display their creations for locals and tourists alike. This invitational event originated as the dream of kite hobbyist Steve O'Brien and as the creation of Larry and Lynn Goodman, former owners of KCRE radio station in Crescent City, California. Beginning in 2001 the Port of Brookings Harbor assumed sponsorship of

A ring-style kite takes to the air at the Southern Oregon Kite Festival.

the festival. In 2006, the kite festival became a nonprofit organization managed by a dedicated group of community volunteers.

The event, which is free to the public (including free parking and a free shuttle bus), offers kite demonstrations featuring everything from classic diamond-style kites to elaborate and incredibly decorative giant inflatables (and many other kinds of kites). Kids can build kites themselves at the free kite-making classes, and a variety of vendors offer not only kites and kite-related merchandise but also other arts and crafts and a variety of local foods. The festival begins with a Friday-night indoor kite-flying demo at the Brooking-Harbor High School gymnasium, then the outdoor events begin Saturday morning at 10 at the harbor along the mouth of the Chetco River (which is also adjacent to lovely Sporthaven Beach).

Sunday begins with the pancake breakfast at the Harbor Fire Hall. Parking is limited at the kite-flying field, but the free shuttle buses run from the spacious parking lot nearby on Lower Harbor Road. Each year, the festival publishes a program (available on the website) that lists many lodging options, but make reservations early; RVers can find spaces very close to the kite field at either Beachfront RV Park, www.beachfrontrvpark.com, or Driftwood RV Park, www.driftwoodrvpark.com, and the area offers several other RV sites.

DOG DAYS OF SUMMER
OREGON COAST BREW FESTIVAL

Newport
Rogue Ales & Spirits, 2320 SE OSU Drive
Second weekend in August
www.rogue.com

Oregon is a decidedly dog-friendly state, and many of its craft breweries welcome our four-legged friends to outdoor seating venues as allowed by state law. So why not honor canine companions by throwing a brew bash specifically for a beloved pup from long ago—Rogue Ales brewmaster John Maier's faithful buddy, the black Labrador aptly named Brewer, who passed away in 2006. In honor of Brewer, Rogue launched Brewer's Memorial Ale Fest, now called the Rogue Dog Days of Summer Oregon Coast Brew Festival, which celebrates dogs perhaps even more than it celebrates ales.

Held at Rogue's main campus on the south side of Yaquina Bay, this two-day festival features a variety of activities for dogs and their owners: cutest wag contest, best dog trick competitions, dog fashion contest, doggy musical chairs, dog wash, dog–owner lookalike contest, dog Olympics, and the ever-popular Brewer lookalike competition. Fittingly, Rogue Brewery donates proceeds from the event, which charges a nominal entry fee and modest fees for beer samples, to local pet charity organizations.

For this unique festival, Rogue invites other regional breweries, so attendees can enjoy more than thirty ales from a dozen or so craft ale producers. Live music entertains guests throughout the event, which runs from 4 pm

It's all about the dogs—and the ales—at the Dog Days of Summer Oregon Coast Brew Festival.

to 10 pm on Friday, and noon to 10 pm on Saturday. Tickets are available at Rogue's website and at the door. One of Oregon's largest and oldest breweries, Rogue is also among the most socially and culturally cognizant and responsible breweries in the state. A complete list of their many special events is available on the brewery website.

In addition to the headquarters in Newport, Rogue Ales & Spirits operates several tap houses in Portland, as well as one in Astoria and one each in Issaquah, Washington, and San Francisco, California. Rogue also has a taphouse and restaurant on the north side of Yaquina Bay on the historic Newport bayfront. Near Independence, Oregon, Rogue operates a cozy and inviting tasting room and farm. In addition to its well-known ales, Rogue crafts lagers, ciders, distilled spirits, and sodas; the brewery's seasonal ales are legion and legendary.

LIGHTHOUSE BREW FESTIVAL

Lincoln City
McMenamins Lighthouse Brewery,
  4157 N Highway 101
Mid-August
www.mcmenamins.com/lighthouse-brew-festival

McMenamins Lighthouse Brewery has been a Lincoln City landmark since it opened in the late 1980s, serving up excellent pub food from a surprisingly deep menu and pouring outstanding ales brewed onsite. Summer is an especially fine time to visit the Lighthouse Brewery: for indoor patrons, sunrays beam comfortably in through the upstairs windows; outside, the upstairs patio looks out over the city, with heaters to fend off the gathering coastal chill as the sun sets.

Better still, high summer brings the annual Lighthouse Brew Festival, in which McMenamins and guest brewers concoct their own distinctive beers for patrons to try, while the Lighthouse staff serves up food specials and offers brewery tours throughout the Saturday event. As part of the annual tradition, the brew fest kicks off weeks earlier with the "Vallancing Act" (named for former Lighthouse Brewer Rob Vallance) during which each participating McMenamins brewer picks a number. Then beer styles are pulled from a Portland Timbers hat to correspond to that number. The brewers are then required to brew an original recipe in that style, which will be served at the festival. Each participating brewery is also asked to submit a tiny image to represent their particular brew.

This collection of "Tiny Brewer Art," always amusing if not befuddling, is displayed in the festival booklet provided to patrons, along with descriptions of the beers. Each year, McMenamins also unveils a new Mighty Beer Atom, an in-house graphic symbol or totem produced by McMenamins staff in varying positions that represents the creative spirit and energy of brewers and brewing. There is no admission fee for the all-day Lighthouse Brew Festival, and all ages are welcome (21 and over to drink).

McMenamins invites guest brewers to concoct special ales for the Lighthouse Brew Festival.

BLACKBERRY ARTS FESTIVAL

Coos Bay
Downtown Coos Bay
Late August
www.blackberryartsfestival.com

Blackberry Arts Festival literally fills the streets of Downtown Coos Bay, with bay area residents coming out in force each year for this alluringly tasty late-summer street fair that, as the name implies, features all kinds of mouthwatering blackberry-inspired treats. But, launched in 1982, the Blackberry Arts Festival is no longer a local secret—each year, many outsiders head for Coos Bay to take in this family-friendly Saturday/Sunday event sponsored by the Coos Bay Downtown Association.

In addition to the yummy blackberry culinary specialties—pies and other pastries, jams, candies, and even wine—the Blackberry Arts Festival also includes a variety of other food vendors, and myriad arts and craft vendors lining Central Avenue between Fourth Street and Bayshore Drive. The art show is juried and features many genres, including painting, printing, jewelry, photography, woodworking, pottery, weaving, and more. Throughout the weekend, live music—the Blackberry Jam—entertains the crowds. The music lineup, sponsored by the local radio station, features a variety of regional artists, and the event also hosts the annual Bay Area Teen Idol semifinals. This buoyant festival also features a variety of special events, changing somewhat over the years. Favorites include the recipe contest and the children's blackberry costume contest and parade.

The Blackberry Arts Festival includes a beer garden, sponsored in recent years by local 7 Devils Brewing, located just two blocks south of the Central Avenue, the festival grounds. A four-block-long stretch of Central Avenue is closed to vehicle traffic for the event, but parking is generally easy to find fairly close by if you arrive early in

Perusing the wares available at the Blackberry Arts Festival in Coos Bay.

the day; the festival runs from 9 am to 6 pm on Saturday, and 10 am to 4 pm on Sunday. A number of Coos Bay restaurants offer blackberry specials during the festival—look for the blackberry character wearing sunglasses in the windows of the participating eateries.

MILL-LUCK SALMON CELEBRATION

North Bend
The Mill Hotel at The Mill Casino,
   3201 Tremont Avenue
Second weekend in September
www.themillcasino.com

For millennia, indeed beginning many thousands of years before even the Egyptian pyramids were built, the fertile Pacific Ocean sustained Native Americans along Oregon's coastline. The marine environment of this coast, south of the massive ice-age ice sheets that covered much of the continent until about 12,000 years ago, provided everything the highly adaptable early Americans needed, including salmon runs so robust we can scarcely conceive of such abundance today. These salmon runs shaped indigenous culture and to this day the Northwest Coast tribes celebrate the fish and their profound significance.

Perhaps nowhere in the region is this connection between salmon and the first peoples so joyously championed as at the Coquille Tribe's free annual Mill Luck Salmon Celebration, held at Mill Luck Casino in North Bend. Salmon Celebration is both educational and entertaining, with a variety of demonstrations and interactive events by tribal vendors and craftspeople.

One of the highlights is the traditional outdoor salmon bake, in which slabs of fresh salmon are fastened to steaks and roasted over a big fire pit in the fashion used for generations

A traditional outdoor salmon bake is a highlight of the Mill-Luck Salmon Celebration.

by the local tribes. Tribal members also demonstrate artforms such as drumming and dancing, compete in a traditional-style canoe race, and offer rides to attendees in their beautifully crafted canoes. The races take place Saturday from 9 am to noon, and on Sunday (weather permitting) guests can experience a canoe ride any time between 11 am and 2 pm.

The salmon bake is ongoing both Saturday and Sunday, and for less than the price of a restaurant dinner, attendees at this family-friendly event enjoy a sumptuous salmon meal. Admission to the salmon dinner includes a Salmon Celebration T-shirt; or for a few dollars less, guests can buy just the meal alone. The baked salmon is plated with a variety of sides. Tickets are sold at the casino's Ko-Kwel Gift Shop; for more information, call (541) 756-8800.

Many—no doubt, most—Oregonians don't realize the significance of their home state in the field of American archeology, but ongoing research continues to demonstrate not only how long people have lived here, but also how widely dispersed they were and how innovative they have always been in adapting to the land and all it offers. Salmon Celebration offers a chance for visitors to better understand native cultures and appreciate the necessity of promoting intact habitats where native salmon can flourish.

GOLD BEACH BREW & ART FESTIVAL

Gold Beach
Curry County Fairgrounds,
    29392 Ellensburg Avenue
Early September
www.goldbeachbrewfest.org

The proliferation of craft ales in Oregon has touched every corner of the state, with brewers willing to dive into the fray even in the smallest communities, thereby adding measurably to the allure of their hometowns. The coast is no exception, and in recent years, breweries have sprouted in every major town, from Astoria to Brookings, and many minor communities as well. Even the beautiful little city of Gold Beach, at the mouth of the mighty Rogue River, now enjoys the ales produced by Arch Rock Brewing Company, one of the annual participants in the Gold Beach Brew & Art Fest held each September at the Curry County Fairgrounds.

With amazing beaches—from the clean, bright sand of Ophir and Bailey Beaches north of town to the sea-stack-studded beaches at Meyers Creek and Sisters Rocks south of town—Gold Beach is an idyllic setting for a brew fest, and while extremely popular with locals, this event also attracts many devotees from afar, in increasing numbers. The modest entry fee to the festival includes a festival-logo beer glass—a prized addition to the brew-fest glass collection for Oregon craft beer aficionados—along with the opportunity to sample ales from about a dozen regional breweries (adult 21 and over only, though minors accompanied by adults can attend).

While checking out ales produced by top brewers in the region, attendees can also peruse the works of many different craftspeople and artists selling their wares and demonstrating their talents, all to the accompaniment of live music performed on two stages, one indoors and one outdoors, throughout the day, with the congenial partylike atmosphere amping up in the late afternoon and evening (the festival runs from noon to 10 pm). Music acts represent a variety of genres—blues, country, classic rock, and more—with the lineup of musicians rotating annually but always including favorite acts from the south coast region and beyond. Bring your dancing shoes, so to speak, or enjoy the music from a comfortable seat at one of the many tables both indoors and out. Food vendors provide a variety of options, and adults and kids alike revel in the display of masterfully restored and maintained vintage automobiles in the classic car show sponsored by Curry County Cruisers.

September is a wonderful time of year in Gold Beach, with the weather typically pleasant and sunny. Lodging options are fairly plentiful in and near town, but make reservations well in advance of the brew fest.

Modest crowds enjoy the under-the-radar Gold Beach Brew & Art Festival.

PACIFIC NORTHWEST BREW CUP

Astoria
Waterfront at the Columbia River Maritime Museum
Last full weekend in September
www.pacificnorthwestbrewcup.com

In a state that seems to throw a craft brew festival every weekend of the year, standing out from the crowd is no easy task, but Astoria's Pacific Northwest Brew Cup does just that. In January, 2010—after the festival's eighth iteration—John Foyston of *The Oregonian* bestowed upon the event his "Best Beer Festival" honors. This three-day beercentric extravaganza centers on sampling more than three dozen craft beers (with wine and cider available as well), and then choosing your favorites—attendees get to vote for two major awards: the People's Choice award and the coveted Thar She Blows award for the first keg that empties. In this latter category, attendees vote with their taste buds—the first keg to run dry is obviously a beer that resonates with the crowd. Each brewery brings one special beer, and the competition is fierce as the brewers always treat attendees to a wide array of outstanding creations.

Sprawling in the spirit of a congenial street party, this lively outdoors event (with tents and umbrella-covered tables to fend off rain) is held on the Waterfront at the Columbia River Maritime Museum, and you can bet the local breweries—Buoy, Fort George, Reach Break—will be there representing the hometown beer scene. Throughout the long weekend, more than a dozen bands take to the stage, providing an outstanding variety of live music, and food carts offer many different options for great eats. Entry to this 21-and-over festival is free, but beer samplers pay a modest fee for their commemorative sampling mug and then $1 each for tasting tokens.

The Pacific Northwest Brew Cup is a fundraising event benefiting the Astoria Downtown Historic District Association, whose mission is to encourage community involvement and

Pacific Northwest Brew Cup in Astoria is among the state's best beer festivals.

investment in preserving the character of Downtown Astoria while promoting its health and future. This multiday festival provides the perfect opportunity for visitors to explore the city in all its character and historic charm, and the association website (www.astoriadowntown.com) includes a downloadable map showing the museums and historical sites. Accommodations in Astoria range from simple motels to elegant B&Bs, and this waterfront town of about 10,000 residents offers a wide range of excellent restaurants—not to mention the local brewpubs. The beautiful beach at Fort Stevens State Park is a short drive west, and Astoria's iconic bridge leads four miles across the mouth of the Columbia to Washington.

BANDON CRANBERRY FESTIVAL

Bandon
Various venues
Early September
www.bandon.com/cranberry-festival

To those unfamiliar with Oregon's south coast, a festival celebrating cranberries might seem a bit peculiar. But Curry and Coos Counties alone produce about 7 percent of the nation's cranberry crop, and Oregon is actually one of just five states that together account for nearly the entire commercial cranberry crop in the country. Cranberry bogs abound in the coastal lowlands in the immediate vicinity of the eclectic, picturesque community of Bandon, where the first

cranberry farms were fledged in the 1890s. Today, some 1,600 acres around Bandon are under cultivation with cranberries, and so central to the local economy are the bright-red berries that in 1947 community leaders launched the first Cranberry Festival. Not coincidentally, the previous year, 1946, was paramount for commercial production of cranberries on the south coast as the Ocean Spray

Bandon Cranberry Festival offers a full slate of great activities for all ages.

cooperative expanded its operations northward from California.

That first year, the Cranberry Festival was composed of the then-labeled "big three events": the festival queen coronation and ball, the Cranberry Bowl high school football game, and the Cranberry Festival dance. The following year, the Cranberry Parade was added, and it has since become perhaps the single most popular aspect of this three-day autumn celebration. The Cranberry Bowl likewise continues its illustrious tradition as a key part of the festival, with Bandon High School pitted against one of its area rivals on Friday night, and the Cranberry Queen coronation likewise remains a key part of the event.

In more modern iterations, however, the Cranberry Festival has added many other events and activities, including the uproarious cranberry-eating contests on the main festival stage, and the much-anticipated Queen of the Kitchen cooking contests in which chefs of all ages whip up their best dishes—which must include cranberries—to compete in various categories, such as appetizers, main dishes, relishes, and of course deserts. Throughout the festival, Cranberry City at Old Town Marketplace is home to dozens of vendors selling many different wares, including art works and crafts, along with many foodstuffs and fresh produce.

Saturday midmorning brings the expansive Cranberry Festival Parade coursing through Old Town Bandon to the delight of countless onlookers, and the vendor market continues throughout the day, long with the cranberry-eating contests, live music, and much more. The Saturday evening Cranberry Court coronation at Sprague Community Theater features young ladies who are vying for the crown delivering speeches and showing off their individual talents—and the queen automatically qualifies as a contestant for Miss Oregon. Among the Sunday events is the all-you-can-eat breakfast at the VFW hall and the popular Cranberry Run (a one-mile run/walk and both 5K and 10K road races). Each year the festival carries a new theme, and activities and events vary to some extent (see the festival website for details).

Bandon is one of the most popular destinations on the south coast and for good reason—it's a charming little town with gorgeous beaches, eclectic shops, a wide variety of nice restaurants, and numerous lodging options (make reservations well in advance for festival weekend accommodations). Parking can be challenging during festival weekend.

BAY AREA FUN FESTIVAL

Coos Bay
Downtown Coos Bay
Third weekend in September
www.bayareafunfestival.com

Just as summer is winding down post-Labor Day, the Coos Bay Downtown Association throws one last bash—the "greatest last party of the summer," as it's billed—in the form of the multipronged Bay Area Fun Festival. Thousands of locals and visitors from afar come to enjoy the sights, sounds, and tastes of beautiful Downtown Coos Bay and surrounding areas for this popular event—and usually at this time of year, in mid-September, the south coast shows off its typically awesome early autumn weather.

The Fun Festival kicks off with what is perhaps its signature event, the bustling Prefontaine Memorial Run, an Oregon State Championship 10K race that attracts many dozens of runners to the hometown of legendary track star Steve Prefontaine, who died tragically at age 24 in 1975, at the height of his career. This memorial race also features a two-mile fun run/walk and a 5K event for high school cross-country teams (the 5K is sanctioned by the Oregon State Athletic Association). All races begin Saturday morning, with their start times staggered. For full details, visit www.prefontainerun.com. Runners and other festival attendees can visit the Prefontaine Memorial Gallery at the Coos Art Museum, the permanent collection of Pre's awards and memorabilia, along with numerous photos highlighting his illustrious career at Marshfield High School, the University of Oregon, and on the international stage.

Early afternoon, after the footraces, the Fun Fest Parade courses up 4th Street and winds through downtown to the delight of throngs of onlookers lining the sidewalks, and on Central Avenue, the huge Fun Festival Vendor Market includes arts, crafts,

The Bay Area Fun Festival is billed as "the greatest last party of the summer."

edibles, and other wares. The festival has a dedicated food court with myriad choices, as well as a beer and wine garden. Live music—the Bay Area Fun Festival RockFest—entertains the masses thanks to local K-DOCK 92.9 radio and a host of sponsors. On Saturday evening, nearly 500 exquisitely restored vintage automobiles make their way through the streets of downtown during the Cruz the Coos event organized by the Coos Bay–North Bend Rotary Club. The festival offers a variety of other events, such as a rock and gem show and a quilt show, and culminates with the popular and entertaining Bay Area Teen Idol finals on Sunday afternoon at the RockFest stage on 4th and Central (the semifinals are held during the Blackberry Arts Festival in August).

The Bay Area Fun Fest is a family-friendly affair, and a great opportunity to explore Coos Bay and the surrounding region—from the many fun restaurants and shops around town to the historic bayfront, to the gorgeous hidden beaches just to the west, near Charleston.

LINCOLN CITY CHOWDER & BREWFEST

Lincoln City
Lighthouse Square
Early September
www.chowderbrewfest.com

Mohava Marie Niemi (1913–1992)—far better known simply as "Mo"—was an institution on the Oregon coast. In the 1940s she opened her first restaurant, on the bayfront in Newport, called Freddie and Mo's, which would morph into Mo's Restaurants. The restaurant soon gained widespread acclaim for its clam chowder, and in the 1970s Mo's hatched the idea of packaging and selling frozen chowder base, greatly expanding its renown. All this hubbub about Mo's clam chowder created—and, to this day, still creates—an almost carnival atmosphere at the original Mo's, where lines of people waiting to be seated meander down the street on busy weekends. Mo's no doubt inspired many other chowder makers, and clam chowder has long been a staple on the Oregon coast, with many independent restaurants—from well-known four-star dinner houses to walk-up food carts—creating their own special recipes.

All of this ardor over clam chowder culminates in the annual Lincoln City Chowder & Brewfest held at Lighthouse Square on the north end of town each autumn: and what better way to explore the diverse world of Oregon clam chowder than with a craft ale in hand on the beautiful Oregon coast? Attendees can sample many different chowders and buy a bowl full of their favorites, pairing the chowder with an ale (or cider or glass of wine) from any of nearly two dozen participating brewers. Live music entertains festival-goers throughout the day, and a variety of games provide

A steaming hot cup of famous Mo's clam chowder.

raucous entertainment, especially the ever-popular giant Jenga. Tickets to the Chowder & Brewfest are available for sale on the event website, which also has a convenient portal to book lodging in Lincoln City. The festival is open to children accompanied by their parents (21 and over only to drink). Conveniently located, the festival venue is a short drive away from beach accesses and the many attractions and activities that make Lincoln City such a popular destination.

STORMY WEATHER ARTS FESTIVAL

Cannon Beach
Various venues
Early November
www.cannonbeach.org/explore/Cannon-Beach-Stormy-Weather-Arts-Festival

More than three decades old and going strong, the Stormy Weather Arts Festival gathers a diverse array of talents to Cannon Beach each November for a weekend of performances, exhibits, and special activities on the beautiful Oregon coast. Cannon Beach fosters a vibrant arts community and is home to a dozen or so galleries and many skilled artists.

Specifics vary somewhat year to year, but popular Stormy Weather Arts Festival events begin with a Friday evening Stormy Weather Arts Benefit Cocktail and Dessert Party featuring skilled jewelry artists and their bedazzling works. The party includes a silent auction and raffle with proceeds benefitting children's art programs in Cannon Beach, including the Coaster Theatre's Coaster Kidz Theatre Camp, the Cannon Beach Arts

Association children's Summer Art Camp, and the Sea Ranch Children's Summer Music Camp.

The Saturday highlights include a concert featuring well-known or up-and-coming musicians at the 200-seat Coaster Theatre Playhouse. This cozy, intimate venue offers outstanding acoustics in an up-close-and-personal setting.

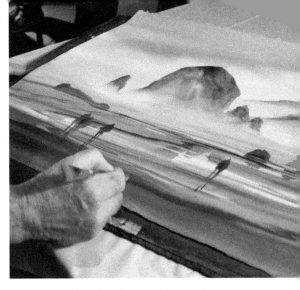

An artist puts the final touches on a depiction of Haystack Rock and Cannon Beach.

Another Saturday event that draws a full house is a lively fashion show called Dancing in the Rain, which features apparel and accessories from local and nationally recognized designers. On Sunday, at the Cannon Beach Community Hall, festival attendees can try local beers and a barbecue lunch to the accompaniment of live blues music.

Throughout the festival, Cannon Beach's galleries host artist receptions and other events, alongside many intriguing exhibits. The talent pool at Stormy Weather includes not only the visual arts (in many different mediums), but also literary and performing arts. Musicians play at a number of small venues throughout Cannon Beach, which is one of the coast's most pedestrian-friendly towns. No matter the weather, simply park at one of the public lots and enjoy the entire festival on foot, checking out not only the galleries and events but the town's hidden treasures in the form of excellent restaurants, wineries and breweries (and even a distillery), and shops of all descriptions.

Even in November—when the weather can indeed be stormy—Cannon Beach is a popular tourist destination, so it pays to make lodging reservations well in advance of the festival.

CENTRAL/
EASTERN
OREGON
FESTIVALS

CENTRAL/EASTERN OREGON FESTIVALS

Two-thirds of Oregon stretches eastward from the Cascade Mountains, but that two-thirds is home to less than 15 percent of the state's population. The eastern side is further geographically divided, colloquially if not strictly geographically, into Central Oregon and Eastern Oregon, as well as additional delineations, namely Southeast Oregon, Northeast Oregon, and the Columbia Gorge. Central Oregon, home of the hyper-popular city of Bend, holds the majority of Eastern Oregon's population.

The point of all this is that many small, agrarian communities in the eastern half of the state hold unique and imaginative festivals. Small-town festivals in Eastern Oregon tend to draw substantially local crowds, which is truly their charm: outsiders are welcomed, embraced by the residents at these wonderful events that celebrate everything from local culture to local produce and more. Ever-busy Bend notwithstanding, Eastern Oregon differs substantially from densely populated Western Oregon. In eastside towns, from the well-known hubs like John Day, Pendleton, La Grande, and Klamath Falls to off-the-radar towns like Condon, Mitchell, Enterprise, and Lakeview (and many others), life is different, slower paced, friendlier. People say hello on the sidewalks and in the stores, stop to talk, happily engage strangers from out of town, and proudly share what they know about their community. They appreciate out-of-towners able to likewise slow down and learn about the local way of life.

Bend, hub of Central Oregon, marches to its own beat, a fast-growing town of people who love outdoor activities and enjoy an eclectic mix of events. Bend (and nearby Redmond and Sisters) isn't really Eastern Oregon, but it's the gateway to Eastern Oregon and offers great festivals. Bend is such a popular tourism destination that reservations are virtually always needed for overnight accommodations, and the earlier the better. Farther east, booking a room tends to be easier, though small towns in Eastern Oregon have more limited lodging options, so for festival weekends, booking a room well in advance is a good idea. If you're festival bound to Eastern Oregon, don't underestimate the drive times, especially for wintertime festivals. Leave plenty early; and plan ample time to visit sights along the way as well as explore the town hosting the festival.

BREWERIES IN THE GORGE
HOLIDAY HANGOVER BREW FEST

Hood River
Elks Lodge, 304 Cascade Avenue
Mid-January
www.breweriesinthegorge.com

Had enough eggnog, hot toddies, and lousy wine picked out by aunts and uncles you barely know? Did the holiday season wear a little thin? Well, the cure is here, at least for craft beer aficionados: the Breweries in the Gorge Holiday Hangover Brew Fest arrives at exactly the right time to replenish your taste buds with the soothing flavors of some of the best ales brewed in Northwest. The Columbia River Gorge is home to more than a dozen great breweries, all of them united by the nonprofit Breweries in the Gorge (BIG) organization that is dedicated to spreading the word about these craft beer producers and the beautiful area in which they reside. The Holiday Hangover Brew Fest is the group's signature wintertime event, held each year in mid-January at the Hood River Elks Lodge.

With live music by top area bands and food concessions from local food carts, this festive party includes every member of BIG, from iconic, longstanding breweries to relative newcomers: Full Sail Brewing, Double Mountain Brewery, Big Horse Brewery, Logsdon Farmhouse Ales, and pFriem Family Brewers, all from Hood River; Thunder Island Brewing in Cascade Locks; Freebridge Brewing and Sedition Brewing in The Dalles; Solera Brewing in Mount Hood; and Backwoods Brewing, Dwinell Country Ales, Everybody's Brewing, Walking Man Brewing, and 54° 40' Brewing Company, all from the Washington side of the Columbia River (expect a few more added to the list as new breweries spring up in this region that is revered by tourists).

Each of the breweries pours a variety of its best beers, including seasonal ales and limited releases, and even ciders. The

Holiday Hangover Brew Fest kicks off Oregon's beer fest season.

admission fee to this 21-and-over event ($25 in recent years) includes a commemorative drinking glass and ten drink tickets. Advance-purchase tickets are available online through Mercury Ticketing (see the event website); admission at the door is cash only. The fest runs from noon to 8 pm on Saturday only. The Elks Lodge has a large parking lot, and several other public lots are located within easy walking distance.

And speaking of walking distance, Downtown Hood River offers all kinds of excellent dining, drinking, and shopping venues, including both Full Sail and Double Mountain breweries and several wine tasting rooms. This picturesque city of about 10,000 people also offers many lodging options. The surrounding area—the heart of the Columbia Gorge—is well worth exploring over a weekend. For information about the area, and help with lodging, consult the Hood River County Chamber of Commerce, www.hoodriver.org.

HIGH GRAVITY EXTRAVAGANZA BREWFEST

Bend
Old Saint Francis School, 700 NW Bond Street
Mid-January
www.mcmenamins.com/high-gravity-brewfest

Craft beer aficionados have almost too many options in Bend; it seems as if a new brewery pops up on a monthly basis. But among all the newcomers are some longstanding favorites, such as iconic Deschutes Brewery, ever-popular Bend Brewing Company, and eclectic Silver Moon Brewing—respectively, the first-, second-, and third-oldest breweries in this destination mountain town, which now has more breweries per capita than any city in Oregon. In 2004, McMenamins joined the fold with its elaborate and beautiful Old Saint Francis School, named for the Catholic school that had formerly occupied the buildings on this large downtown property, which now—in typical McMenamins eclectic and artistic panache—features multiple hotel buildings, theater, bathhouse, restaurant, and several bars.

It also hosts one of Oregon's must-do brew fests, a midwinter affair called High Gravity Extravaganza, in which big, bad, bold, deep-bodied beers take center stage—center stage being the four big fire pits on the property. Yes, it's January in Central Oregon, but the heart of this brew fest is outdoors in the cold and maybe the snow, as attendees sample a variety of beers (tasting punch cards are inexpensive and you can pay by the sample), enjoy live music, and talk shop with the brewers themselves, from both McMenamins and a who's who of other Bend and Central Oregon breweries. Each brewer either creates a special high-gravity beer

Bold, high-octane ales take center stage at High Gravity Extravaganza Brewfest.

for the festival or tinkers with an existing concoction, and festival-goers get to vote for their favorites to crown a People's Choice award winner.

The festival moniker—High Gravity—refers to a brewing term used to define the relative density of a beer's wort (the sweet infusion of ground malt or other grain before fermentation) relative to water; a beer's gravity is a measure of its density at various stages of fermentation. Original gravity is a measure of fermentable and nonfermentable substances in the wort pre-fermentation, and a high-gravity beer refers to a brew with higher alcohol content and a more robust and complex flavor profile. As beer writer Andy Sparhawk explains, "While gravity is important to a brewer, beer fans can benefit from understanding it too. As a beer enthusiast, an understanding of gravity will help you make informed decisions when choosing a beer if styles are not provided. You can infer that a stout with an OG of 1.080 likely has a stronger ABV than a stout at 1.044. A craft beer described as 'high gravity' is referring to the strength in alcohol, a detail that adds to the beer's character."

OREGON WINTERFEST

Bend
Old Mill District
Mid-February
http://bendoregonfestivals.com/winterfest/

With a portion of the proceeds benefiting Big Brothers Big Sisters of Central Oregon, the annual Oregon Winterfest celebrates what Central Oregon does better than just about anywhere in the state: offer up incredible winters complete with unbeatable scenery and endless options for action and entertainment.

Held at Bend's thriving Old Mill District, Winterfest offers live music, incredible ice carving, fire pit competition, the popular 10 Barrel Rail Jam ski and snowboard competition, a bustling fine art and food marketplace, the OMSI Kids

The mesmerizing firepit at the Oregon Winterfest, held in February at Bend's Old Mill District

Area with many fun activities (behind the Les Schwab Amphitheater), numerous excellent food and beverage options, and the Winterfest Wine Walk in which attendees can stroll along a designated path and sample wine along the way at numerous Old Mill businesses. Each year, about one month prior to the big bash, a Winterfest Fire King and Ice Queen are chosen through a theatrical dating-game improvisational performance, and the couple then presides over Winterfest, as well as making numerous public appearances prior to the festival.

Winterfest also offers the ebullient Kids Hot Cocoa Run, in which festival princes and princesses must complete an interactive course with stops where they add ingredients to create the perfect cup of hot cocoa. In addition, Winterfest includes a themed fun run—the Royal Run—that courses through the Old Mill District, with surprises along the way. Runners can register online or the day prior in person at the festival information tent. This three-day wintertime extravaganza runs from 5 to 10 pm on Friday, 11 am to 10 pm on Saturday, and 11 am to 6 pm on Sunday. Days are short in February, and the nighttime hours at Winterfest are magical, especially if snowfall makes an appearance, rendering the entire music-laden scene nothing short of bedazzling. Winterfest is extremely popular, drawing thousands of people, so get tickets (inexpensive) in advance via the festival website.

WINTER WINGS FESTIVAL

Klamath Falls
Oregon Institute of Technology, 3201 Campus Drive
 (event headquarters)
Mid-February
www.winterwingsfest.org

The Klamath Basin is justifiably famous as one of the best birdwatching areas in the West, anchored by a vast National Wildlife Refuge system that includes refuges in both Oregon and across the border in California. Thousands upon thousands of migratory birds—most notably waterfowl—use the basin's sprawling wetlands and agrarian lands as stopovers during both spring and fall; many other species nest in the region, which is composed of numerous habitat types, from open water and marshlands to forested highlands and high-desert steppe. This beautiful area is the perfect place for Oregon's biggest bird and birding celebration, the four-day Winter Wings Festival, held each February in and around Klamath Falls since 1980 and produced via tremendous volunteer effort by members of the Klamath Basin Audubon Society, with support from sponsors, grants, and participant registration fees. Proceeds from the Winter Wings Festival support local grants to teachers and other entities for outdoor education and community nature-related projects.

This congenial festival occurs at precisely the time massive flocks of snow and Ross's geese—starkly white until they take flight en masse and flash black wingtips—occupy fields in the area, joined in the basin by huge flocks of tundra swans, up to two dozen duck species, and myriad raptors, including lots of bald eagles. One of the highlights of Winter Wings is the lineup of field trips that take participants to key birding sites to see the winged marvels that make this area so special. These birding forays take many forms, with outings

Snow geese take flight near Klamath Falls, site of Winter Wings Festival.

of varying lengths to numerous locations throughout the area, with some excursions focusing on particular species and others seeking to find as many different birds as possible. Specifics vary annually, but the festival field trips—some free, others requiring a fee, and all requiring registration—offer something for everyone. Another key component of Oregon's largest bird festival is the intriguing schedule of seminars and workshops covering many topics, including bird identification, photography, ecology, and conservation.

Each year, the festival features expert speakers presenting both workshops and keynote presentations. Keynoters are announced during the summer prior to the event, and the program schedule is released around mid-November. Online registration begins the second week of December, and attendees should register as early as possible because space fills quickly in the various field trips and workshops. All registration information is available on the festival website; make sure to check the website for updates on the timing of online registration.

Winter Wings is headquartered at Oregon Institute of Technology, the location for most of the workshops and presentations, as well as the robust vendor section, featuring artists, photographers, craftspeople, authors, conservation groups, and various local businesses and agencies. The festival headquarters is also the scene of Winter Wings Bird Central, where all species sighted during the festival are logged by participants. Volunteers at Bird Central can help attendees identify birds, offer suggestions on where to go, and provide directions to prime birding sites. Winter Wings also features a popular bird photography contest, open to anyone, featuring birds photographed during the festival dates (full contest details are listed on the festival website). In fact, bird and nature photography is a central theme of the festival, with a variety of programming—field trips, workshops, and expert speakers—dedicated to this popular art form.

HOOD RIVER HARD-PRESSED CIDER FEST

Hood River
3315 Stadelman Drive
Late April
www.hoodriver.org/cider-fest/

Hood River County is renowned for its pears, apples, and cherries, with orchards sprawling over the verdant, rolling hills of this pastoral countryside. Each April, the county celebrates the blossoming of the trees—when the orchards paint the county in vibrant pinks and ivory whites—with the monthlong Hood River Valley Blossom Time. Among the many events and activities is the daylong, late-April Hood River Hard-Pressed Cider Fest, which highlights the burgeoning local cider industry and features more than two dozen cideries from the Columbia Gorge and beyond pouring more than fifty different ciders.

Fittingly, this jovial and bustling festival is held in the heart of the orchard country, amid the blooming fruit trees, at the state-of-the-art Mount Defiance Cold Storage facility (about eight miles south of town via SR 30), which transforms into an ideal event center for the day. Craft ciders have become so popular in Oregon that this relatively new festival, launched in 2014, draws near-elbow-to-elbow crowds during the peak afternoon hours, but rows of picnic tables set up under the storage facility loading dock roof provide ample seating, and lines for samples and glass pours at the various cidery booths go quickly as likeminded enthusiasts meld in conversation. Throughout the festival, local and regional bands provide live music, and local restaurants and caterers provide delectable food options. Drinking is for the 21-and-over crowd of course, but children are welcome and a special kid's area includes a bouncy house and other activities (dogs are not allowed).

The Hood River Hard-Pressed Cider Fest highlights one of the most intriguing aspects of the craft cider industry in the Northwest: hard ciders (alcoholic ciders) are ubiquitous of course, but Oregon cideries are fermenting just about every fruit that hangs from a tree and grows on a bush. From the well-established cideries to innovative newcomers,

Musicians entertain cider aficionados at the Hood River Hard-Pressed Cider Fest.

Oregon cider-heads revel in the diversity, with hard apple ciders made in countless iterations and many other ciders made from pears, blackberries, raspberries, apricots, peaches, cherries, strawberries, citrus fruits, pineapples, and watermelon. And it gets even wilder with prickly pear cactus fruits, rhubarb, ginger, kiwi berries, and hot peppers. Creative fermenters even concoct a variety of spiced ciders, not to mentioned hopped ciders, and ciders aged in oak barrels. There's no end in sight to the creative diversity and there's no better place to experience it than the Hood River Hard-Pressed Cider Fest.

HARNEY COUNTY MIGRATORY BIRD FESTIVAL

Burns
Burns High School and Harney County
   Chamber of Commerce office
Early April
www.migratorybirdfestival.com

Covering 10,226 square miles but with a population of about 7,500 people, Southeast Oregon's Harney County is the state's largest county and the county with the lowest population density. It is also home to Malheur National Wildlife Refuge, one of the most venerated birdwatching areas in the West, along with numerous other outstanding birding sites. The county includes agrarian valleys and shallow wetlands in and around the refuge and near the county seat of Burns, these vast areas in total serving as a major migration stop for myriad bird species and an important nesting region for many more.

    Birding enthusiasts come from throughout the nation to visit Malheur and the other hotspots in Harney County, and the Burns-based Harney County Chamber of Commerce throws a terrific birding bash each spring in the form of the Harney County Migratory Bird Festival. The event occurs at a time when white geese—snow geese and their smaller but nearly identical cousins, Ross's geese—are staging by the thousands in the area, providing a spectacle for birders. The sight of several thousand white geese with black wingtips taking flight in unison is surreal. Likewise, the county wetlands and fields fill with a variety of other species—ducks of numerous kinds, other species of geese, shorebirds, Sandhill cranes, and more.

The festival begins on Thursday evening at the Chamber of Commerce in Downtown Burns, with a meet-and-greet event for attendees to mingle with festival tour leaders, authors, and organizers. But the festival headquarters is actually Burns High School, where the gymnasium houses vendors, including artists, photographers, birding and conservation organizations, and

Harney County Migratory Bird Festival celebrates one of the state's best birding regions.

more. On Friday and Saturday, birding tours (register online in advance) leave from the high school first thing in the morning, heading out to a variety of locations near and far—Malheur National Wildlife Refuge, the east side of Steens Mountain, Silvies Valley, and other hotspots. Each tour is led by expert birders who know the area well. The tours arrive back at the high school late in the afternoon, and the vendor show remains open into the evenings. Saturday evening culminates with a speaker dinner program (tickets available in advance). Tour locations, prices, and details are listed on the event website early each spring. Burns and conjoined Hines offer about half a dozen hotels, but reserve a room early, as several hundred people usually attend the festival; visit the chamber website, www.harneycounty.com for lodging information and other local details.

NORTHWEST CHERRY FESTIVAL

The Dalles
Downtown area
Late April
thedalleschamber.com/northwest-cherry-festival/

Showcasing the agricultural and Western heritage of The Dalles—an historic Oregon community on the banks of the Columbia River—the Northwest Cherry Festival was launched in 1979, though its roots date back to 1940, when a local woman, Helen Spickerman, was chosen as Cherry Queen to represent the city and one of its most important products at the Rose Parade in Portland.

World War II interrupted the idea thereafter until 1960 when the Wasco County Fruit and Produce League and the Washington Fruit Commission, in conjunction with The Dalles Area Chamber of Commerce, created and promoted a new symbol of the industry, the Cherry Sweetheart. Nowadays, this popular and extravagant

A beautifully restored vintage delivery truck at the Northwest Cherry Festival.

weekend-long celebration envelopes the city's wonderful downtown district and features myriad events and attractions for all ages.

The centerpiece of the Cherry Festival is the largest parade in the Columbia Gorge on Saturday morning, featuring the Cherry Festival Royalty with King Bing and Queen Anne, who are crowned that morning. The festival also features a classic car show, a lip sync contest, great local live music, a carnival by Davis Shows Northwest, and—naturally—a chance to sample cherries and cherry products of many descriptions, as well as peruse the wares of a wide array of vendors. Over the years the mix of activities has changed a bit but always includes a superb lineup of events for all ages, including a variety of unique highlights such as the Once Upon a Cherry Faire, a reenactment and demonstration of life in the Middle Ages, including dancing, archery, fighting, clothing, food, music, arts, and more, all produced by the Society for Creative Anachronism. A number of events—such as the Cherry Festival Softball Tournament hosted by Wasco County Parks and Recreation and the annual Cherry of a Ride recreational bicycle ride sponsored by Saint Mary's Academy—are not officially part of the festival but are associated with it to create a comprehensive weekend extravaganza with something for everyone.

The festival begins Friday afternoon, and from 6:30 to 9 pm the Family Pit Party (a family dance party) is ongoing downtown. Saturday morning kicks off with the Cherry Festival Breakfast, beginning at 7:30 am, and the crowning of the Cherry Festival Royalty, as well as the Northwest Cherry Festival Run (10K). The Northwest Cherry Festival Parade begins at 10 am and draws throngs of cheerful onlookers; a caravan of motorcyclists precedes the parade in the Teddy Bear Run, in which riders carry teddy bears they donate to the local emergency services for children in difficult circumstances. Saturday evening brings the finals of the Northwest Cherry Idol live singing competition.

The Northwest Cherry festival is a free family-friendly extravaganza (the Davis Shows Carnival requires purchase of a ticket, either at the gate or in advance at The Dalles Area Chamber of Commerce at 404 West 2nd Street). The Dalles, a congenial town of about 15,000 people, offers a wonderful array of dining options, lodging options, and attractions; several excellent breweries and wineries, and a variety of intriguing shops, are located in the downtown area where the Cherry Festival is held.

LADD MARSH BIRD FESTIVAL

La Grande
Ladd Marsh Wildlife Area
Weekend after Mother's Day
www.friendsofladdmarsh.org/bird-festival-2

The annual family-friendly Ladd Marsh Bird Festival celebrates birdwatching activities, the diversity of birds, and the excellent wildlife habitat at the Oregon Department of Fish and Wildlife's 6,000-acre Ladd Marsh Wildlife Area a few miles southeast of La Grande. Scheduled to coincide with the peak of spring migration, the event provides a terrific opportunity for birders both novice and expert to view copious numbers of birds that stop at the marsh and surrounding areas—and during the weekend festival, participants enjoy access to portions of the wildlife area normally closed to the public.

Hosted by the all-volunteer nonprofit Friends of Ladd Marsh along with numerous agency and business partners, the festival begins Friday evening with a presentation by an expert guest speaker, and attendees can register for workshops and field trips then or any time during the weekend (the festival is free). The Friday evening kickoff (at Union County Senior Center in La Grande) allows participants to peruse vendor booths, enjoy live music, meet festival volunteers, and plan weekend activities. To register for the festival, visit the Friends of Ladd Marsh website, which also includes a festival schedule and map.

A Yellow-headed Blackbird at Ladd Marsh.

On Saturday and Sunday, registration opens at 6 am at the Tule Lake Public Access site on Peach Road at the east side of wildlife area. Participants can visit six different birding stations set up at various prime locations and staffed by experts who help point out and identify various species and provide lots of interesting information. Volunteers also lead both on- and offsite field trips to a variety of nearby locations—in past years, offsite excursions have included visits to well-known birding hotspots such as Rhinehart Canyon north of Imbler and the Spring Creek Great Gray Owl Management Area west of La Grande. The Ladd Marsh Bird Festival features a variety of events specifically for children, including arts-and-crafts activities, such as birdhouse building, as well as a special Junior Birder Program in which kids can visit various educational stations, complete various activities, and earn a Junior Birder badge.

In addition to seeing abundant ducks and other waterfowl, festival attendees often enjoy glimpses of more secretive marsh inhabitants, such as American bitterns, Virginia rails, and sora rails, and with the festival scheduled for prime time during spring migration, birders often find many different species of songbirds, especially on field trips to outlying hotspots, such as Rhinehart Canyon.

AMERICA'S GLOBAL VILLAGE FESTIVAL

Ontario
Lions Park
First Saturday in June
www.ontariochamber.com

As unlikely as it may seem, the far-eastern town of Ontario annually hosts one the state's most interesting and educational cultural festivals. On the first Saturday of each June, the America's Global Village Festival brings together a host of diverse cultures, all of which have helped make America the multicultural wonderland of the world. Hosted by the Ontario Chamber of Commerce, this kaleidoscopic event features authentic cultural villages—

African, Basque, German, Hawaiian, Irish, Japanese, Mexican, Native American, pioneer, and Scottish.

At each village, attendees can sample and purchase traditional foods, study and purchase arts and crafts native to that culture, and talk with village members dressed in traditional attire; each village also produces cultural demonstrations and free youth activities. And all the villages offer copious information about their culture, making this a wonderful all-ages educational opportunity. Many of these cultures continue to thrive in the region

Mexican theater at the America's Global Village Festival in Ontario.

today and most left indelible proverbial footprints through the history of the Pacific Northwest. The America's Global Village Festival provides a unique opportunity to learn about the history and customs of diverse peoples, and how they have both maintained their unique identities and contributed to the enrichment of our society as a whole.

The festival begins with a parade through Lions Park, in which all the different cultures represented dress in authentic attire, and then throughout the day a main stage features ongoing performances that, over the years, have included Hawaiian, Mexican, Basque, German, and Native American dancers. A tradition of the festival, the Scottish Highland Games are held at the festival and are ushered in by a performance by the Boise Highlanders Scottish Bagpipers, which draws throngs of onlookers. The traditional Scottish Heavy Athletics events are central to the games and include iconic and historical contests such as the caber toss, stone throw, and sheaf toss. The games start midmorning on Saturday, then the festival itself opens at 11 am. Free admission to the event includes a passport to carry to each village for a stamp—kids with full passports earn prizes. This congenial and educational festival, launched in 1990, earned an Ovation Award from the Oregon Festivals and Events Association in 2013.

THE LITTLE WOODY BARREL-AGED BEER, CIDER & WHISKEY FESTIVAL

Bend, Medford
Deschutes Historical Museum, Harry & David Field
September, May
www.thelittlewoody.com

A multicity festival celebrating the ever-growing enthusiasm and excitement for small-batch wood-aged beers, spirits, and ciders dreamt up by regional brewers, the Little Woody Barrel-Aged Beer, Cider & Whiskey Festival was first launched in Bend in 2009, and has since spread to include Little Woody fests in Medford. With an easily recognizable gnome as the festival icon, Little Woody brings together an eclectic collection of libations and gleeful connoisseurs who enjoy sampling them. Of the impressive array of beers, whiskies, and other offerings, they all have one thing in common: they've spent time in barrels.

While whiskey is traditionally aged in oak barrels, Oregon craft brewers continue to experiment with barrel-aged ales, including beers finished in x-bourbon casks, x-wine casks, x-whiskey casks, new oak barrels, and even x-cognac barrels—and every year brings a new idea for barrel-aged beers. In short, any barrel that's previously held any kind of wine or spirit is fair game for Oregon brewers, and Little Woody brings a bunch of the latest and the greatest, from breweries both big and small, into one big, congenial party (or rather, three big, congenial parties). In addition to sampling many beers and ciders, Little Woody attendees can also taste a variety of whiskies, both ryes and bourbons, all to the accompaniment of live

Little Woody celebrates barrel-aged ales, ciders, and whiskey in two different Oregon cities.

music; local food vendors offer a variety of excellent eats.

Little Woody has proven to be a big hit, not only with the buoyant crowds but also with local breweries, and each year many in-town favorites fill out the vendor list, joining a handful of popular ale makers from throughout the region. Each of them brings the deeply flavored, multilayered beers that define the barrel-aged genre.

Little Woody runs Friday from late afternoon until 10 pm, and Saturday from noon to 10 pm. Modestly priced tickets to the event are available at the gate, but Little Woody draws substantial crowds, so advance ticket purchase assures you'll get in, and advance-purchase tickets (see the event website) are discounted. Paid entry includes a commemorative tasting glass. A tasting package, also modestly priced, includes a glass and eight tasting tokens, and the VIP package for just a few dollars more gets you a VIP glass, ten tasting tokens, and a coveted Little Woody T-shirt, along with early Friday entry. Individual tasting tokens are $1 each, and tastes cost two to five tokens each.

The Medford (May) and Bend (September) Little Woody Festivals are held outdoors. Medford's Little Woody is held at Harry & David Field; the Bend Little Woody is held at the Deschutes Historical Museum.

DEAN HALE WOODPECKER FESTIVAL

Sisters and surrounding area
Various venues
Early June
www.ecaudubon.org/dean-hale-woodpecker-festival

Organized by the East Cascades Audubon Society, the Dean Hale Woodpecker Festival brings together birdwatching enthusiasts from all walks of life to celebrate the woodpecker-rich woodlands of the Deschutes National Forest near Sisters. This region is home to eleven of the state's twelve species of woodpecker, making it one of the best woodpecker-watching areas in the United States. The forested east slope of the Cascades near Sisters has suffered many wildfires over the years, and while the burnt timber and scared landscape left by these conflagrations may seem unsightly, they are a major reason for the preponderance of woodpeckers in the area because dead, burnt snags provide excellent feeding and nesting sites for woodpeckers.

Common species include red-naped, red-breasted, and Williamson's sapsuckers; white-headed woodpeckers; hairy and downy woodpeckers; and northern flickers. Less common but almost always seen by festival field-trip participants are pileated, black-backed, three-toed, and Lewis's woodpeckers. Named after Dean Hale who was tragically killed in a car wreck in 2012, the festival is part of Hale's legacy as a birder par excellence and consummate conservationist and teacher. The festival organizers—all volunteers—are dedicated to sharing their enthusiasm in helping attendees have a great time while seeing many different birds, including, of course, the woodpeckers.

The Pileated Woodpecker is among the stars of the Dean Hale Woodpecker Festival.

Although headquartered in Sisters, the family-friendly woodpecker festival sends birding field trips out to locations both near and far (and in the process typically racks up a total of some 200 species of birds seen). Distant locations include Summer Lake and the Ochoco Mountains; but most field trips head for known birding hotspots in the forests near Sisters. Participants pay a fee for each field trip, with proceeds benefiting the many great conservation and education projects of the East Cascades Audubon Society. Most field trips require some hiking (up to a mile), sometimes over somewhat rough terrain, but the festival also offers vehicle-based field trips for people with limited mobility. Popular special trips include bluebird banding and the evening "Owl Prowl" to listen for and hopefully see not only owls but common poorwills. The festival also features a Saturday-evening social held in Sisters (see website for location and time). Registration for the festival opens April 1, and it's wise to register and select field trips right away as group sizes are limited.

Sisters offers several lodging options (see www.sisterscountry.com), but rooms tend to sell out every weekend during the summer, so make reservation ahead of time. If you prefer camping, Sisters Creekside Campground is conveniently located on the east end of town, and several US Forest Service campground in the area offer not only secluded camping but immediate and outstanding access to prime woodpecker habitat. These include Cold Springs Campground, Indian Ford Campground, and Jack Creek Campground. For details, consult the Sisters Ranger District of Deschutes National Forest, (541) 549-7700 (offices at the west end of Sisters).

RHUBARB FESTIVAL (AKA HIGH DESERT RHUBARB FESTIVAL)

La Pine
L&S Gardens, 50808 S Huntington Road
Mid-June
www.lsgardens.com/rhubarb_festival.html

If you grew up with rhubarb pie, you might not realize that rhubarb is hardly a one-trick pony, and Oregon's only rhubarb festival illuminates the versatility of this herbaceous perennial. Rhubarb is not only useful in many different foodstuffs but also intriguing in that its leaves are actually poisonous while the reddish-colored stocks are edible. These stocks look a lot like celery stocks in general shape, but rhubarb and celery are unrelated and rhubarb is known for its tart flavor. Rhubarb tends to be hardy and able to thrive in colder climate zones; it is generally harvested in late spring and early summer, and Oregon is one of the key states for growing rhubarb. Its culinary use is rather recent, dating back to nineteenth-century Great Britain, where it was a popular ingredient in deserts and for making wine.

Since then, rhubarb has found its way into many different edibles and some nonedibles, which is the nexus for the Rhubarb Festival. Attended annually by about 2,000 people and hosted by author, master gardener, and rhubarb expert Linda Stephenson at her L&S Gardens in La Pine, the Rhubarb Festival (aka High

Linda Stephenson is the host of La Pine's Rhubarb Festival.

Desert Rhubarb Festival) features rhubarb served in every imaginable incarnation—be sure to arrive hungry.

This popular event, in partnership with the community and its many nonprofits, features dozens of vendors selling myriad rhubarb products and many other wares, live music throughout the day, a rhubarb dessert contest, a rhubarb main-dish cook-off, and even a rhubarb beer home-brew competition (with proceeds donated to one of the nonprofits). Admission only requires a donation of at least one canned food good per person (as a donation to a local nonprofit), but bring plenty of cash for nominal tasting fees and irresistible goods, both edible and otherwise, available from the eclectic array of vendors.

La Pine offers a variety of lodging options, Sunriver and Bend are a short distance north, campgrounds abound in the surrounding Deschutes National Forest, and the several RV campgrounds are within easy reach of the festival. For local information, consult the La Pine Chamber of Commerce, (541) 536-9771, www.lapine.org.

4 PEAKS MUSIC FESTIVAL

Bend
Stevenson Ranch, 21085 Knott Road
Mid-June (Summer Solstice)
www.4peaksmusic.com

In a state brimming with alluring music festivals, the annual 4 Peaks Music Festival held near Bend stands out from the crowd not only for its diverse lineup of outstanding music acts and the family-friendly vibe, but also for its venue at the foot of the postcard-pretty Cascades and their snow-capped volcanic peaks in Central Oregon. 4 Peaks' mission is to provide a multiday music event in beautiful Central Oregon, featuring an array of eclectic, national, regional, and local bands for music enthusiasts, community members, and families. Oregon's premier craft music festival not only features outstanding live music but also grand views, grassy fields, a large late-night tent, "chill" areas, and a huge selection of vendors (including local craft beers)—it's among the must-do music scenes in the Northwest.

Launched in 2007—by Central Oregon locals who had a unique vision—4 Peaks Music Festival showcases an impressive, inspiring lineup of musicians, beginning on Thursday evening and running through Sunday.

Headline musicians take the stage throughout each day—two stages actually, a main stage and a tent stage—with other acts performing tweener sets. The music rocks on unabated, featuring myriad genres and an amazing pool of talent, with some two dozen bands and solo artists featured each year. Many notable acts have graced the 4 Peaks stages over the years—moe., Railroad Earth, Jackie Greene, Chris Robinson Brotherhood, Robben Ford, the Jeff Austin

Gorgeous Central Oregon weather awaits attendees at 4 Peaks Music Festival.

Band, Poor Man's Whiskey, Dumpstaphunk, Carolyn Wonderland, Greensky Bluegrass, MarchFourth Marching Band, The Mother Hips, Nicki Bluhm and the Gramblers, Fruition, Ashleigh Flynn, and many more. The event website announces the lineup each spring.

With its spacious, scenic setting, 4 Peaks accomplishes the rare feat of seamlessly blending a high-spirited, family-friendly music-party scene with a chilled-out, intimate atmosphere—it's old-school Oregon, blending great talent with a routinely awesome crowd in an amazing setting. The festival features a dedicated activity-rich kid's area called "Kidlandia" (and 4 Peaks is free for kids up to 10 years old), and attendees can opt for ticket packages that include RV spots (tent/car camping is free). For ticket information and purchase, along with all festival details, visit the 4 Peaks website. Other than service animals, pets are not allowed, but 4 Peaks offers a comprehensive list of local boarding facilities—of great help to people traveling to Central Oregon for the event. Above all, buy your tickets early, well ahead of the festival—4 Peaks Music Festivals has gained a tremendous following and what once was something of a Central Oregon secret among festival aficionados has blossomed into one of the state's best music events.

LAKE OF THE WOODS BEER FEST

Klamath Falls
Lake of the Woods Mountain Lodge & Resort
Mid-June
www.lakeofthewoodsresort.com

Sitting at nearly 5,000 feet at the crest of the Cascade Range in Southern Oregon, 1,146-acre Lake of the Woods gleams and glitters in the summer sun, reflecting snow-capped 9,495-foot Mount McLoughlin to the north and framed by the looming bulk of nearby 7,350-foot Brown Mountain rising off the west shore. Located just off State Route 140 about halfway between Medford and Klamath Falls, the lake is a major attraction for outdoors enthusiasts who are drawn here by the alluring scenic beauty—and if ever there was a perfect place for a summertime beer festival, this is it.

Each June, Lake of the Woods Mountain Lodge & Resort brings in a variety of regional brewers for the Lake of the Woods Beer Fest. First established in the 1920s as a fishing camp, the lodge now features numerous cabins, a general store, RV sites, the popular Lake House Restaurant & Bar, and a full-service marina. The beer fest runs from midafternoon through midevening, and the modestly priced event ticket includes six tasting tickets (age 21 and over) and a festival logo beer glass; additional tasting tickets are available for purchase. Live music entertains the modest crowds and festival goers can buy tickets for the sumptuous BBQ buffet prepared by the Lake House Restaurant.

If the incredible mountain setting weren't enough of a draw, this event provides an opportunity to sample ales produced by some of Southern Oregon's small craft brewers, such as Klamath Basin Brewing and Walkabout Brewing, both of which have attended in years past, and beer aficionados can buy a

Ice cold ales stand ready at Lake of the Woods Beer Fest.

pint of their favorite brew and enjoy the summer sun and incredible views on the resort grounds at the restaurant. If you need a break from beers, try one of the many creative cocktails available in the rustic bar.

Although Lake of the Woods is a fairly easy drive from Medford or Klamath Falls, the perfect way to enjoy this Saturday event is to stay at the resort, but make reservations well in advance; in addition, the US Forest Service operates two campgrounds on Lake of the Woods, both just minutes away from the resort.

WATERSHED FESTIVAL

Enterprise
Wallowa County Fairgrounds, 668 NW 1st Street
Last Friday in June
www.wallowaresources.org

Watershed Festival, a wonderful outdoors event, provides an outstanding opportunity for people of all ages to learn about the many different organizations that serve Wallowa County in myriad ways. Each year, the festival gathers about three dozen local and regional organizations that set up booths with a variety of displays, interactive activities, and educational programs aimed at sharing knowledge about what they do and about the region's wildlife, natural resources, people, and the local way of life in this idyllic mountain valley.

Throughout the day, Wallowa Valley Music Alliance provides live music by local artists and local Future Farmers of America students prepare a variety of foods. Kids love this one-day event because they can engage in numerous hands-on activities, including a fun scavenger hunt in which they win prizes after collecting stickers and facts about Wallowa County. Festival specifics vary annually to some extent, but programs often include the opportunity to build bluebird houses, which the builders can take home; fish for and tag rainbow trout courtesy of Nez

Watershed Festival in Enterprise features many hands-on activities for kids.

Perce Tribe Fisheries; learn how to identify animals by their tracks and scat; learn about trees and other plants; make paper; get a close-up, educational look at hawks, eagles, and owls in a live raptor exhibit; and try your hand at lumberjack games, and much more.

The festival, held on the last Friday in June, is free to attend and runs from 11 am to 4 pm. Plan to spend the day, especially if you bring kids. Free lunch of hot dogs, chips, and fruit is provided by the event organizer, Wallowa Resources. Watershed Festival draws together a long list of sponsors, including local businesses, various nonprofits, and government agencies. Wallowa Resources is a local nonprofit whose mission is to implement innovative solutions that help the people of Wallowa County and the Intermountain West sustain and improve their communities and their lands by promoting watershed health, stabilizing and strengthening the natural-resource-based economy, and broadening community understanding of the ties between environmental health and community health of Wallowa County. Though a local celebration, the Watershed Festival embraces visitors, providing a unique and joyous, fun-filled event where people from near and far can learn why this remarkable corner of Oregon is so special.

WHEELER COUNTY BLUEGRASS FESTIVAL

Fossil
Wheeler County Courthouse Lawn, 701 Adams Street
Late June to early July
www.wheelercountybluegrass.org

Wheeler County, they say, is the only county in Oregon with more horses than people, and in this case, "they" are no doubt correct. This expansive mountainous county sprawls across some 1,700 square miles but is home to only about 1,400 residents. Fossil, with a population of about 500, is the county seat and was named by Thomas B. Hoover, the town's first postmaster. Fossil sits far from the state's major thoroughfares—you have to want to go there.

And when you arrive, slow down; nothing really happens fast in this region—the residents, whether townsfolk or ranch people, always seem happy to chat, offer directions, or provide information. Emulate them and embrace the friendly rural atmosphere.

Annually over the first full weekend in July, Fossil hosts the Wheeler County Bluegrass Festival, which draws remarkably talented professional musicians from throughout the region. Held at the courtyard of the beautiful and historic Wheeler County Courthouse, the festival is free of charge, sponsored by local businesses, agencies,

Up close and personal with the musicians at the Wheeler County Bluegrass Festival.

and organizations. Attendees can partake in impromptu jam sessions, enjoy the festival parade, and even gain valuable instruction from professional musicians who lead free instructional workshops on instruments they play, and with each instrument having a dedicated class, the courthouse lawn can literally host banjo instruction in one corner, a bass instruction across the courtyard, and so on. These instructional sessions vary from year to year, depending on the performing bands and the instruments they play—attendees are encouraged to bring their instruments regardless of skill level. Moreover, the festival holds a popular "Fossil Song Contest" in which contestants sing original, unpublished songs about some feature of the local area.

It's a good idea to bring your own chair—fold-up beach/camp chairs are ideal; camping is available within easy walking distance at the fairgrounds and at the local high school. Fossil has one motel and a variety of B&B-type lodging options, as well as two restaurants and a coffee shop/deli. The John Day Fossil Beds National Monument is about an hour southeast via State Route 19.

MINER'S JUBILEE

Baker City
Geiser Pollman Park, 1723 Madison Street
Third weekend in July
www.minersjubilee.com

Baker City in far Eastern Oregon enjoys a rich Old West history: the discovery of gold in the region in 1861 spurred a gold rush and the birth of

Try your hand at gold panning at Miner's Jubilee in Baker City.

Baker City, which began with a saloon, hotel, and blacksmith shop. In 1865, the town was platted; it became the county seat in 1868, and was officially incorporated as a city in 1874. All the while mining boomed in the nearby mountains, drawing every imaginable kind of character to the bustling town. In 1884, the Oregon Shortline Railroad reached Baker City, and as described by the *Oregon Blue Book*, "By the 1890s the city gained a reputation as the 'Denver of Oregon.' During this period, Baker City was one of the more colorful towns in the Pacific Northwest as miners, ranchers, cowboys, and sheepherders mingled with gamblers and dance hall girls. By 1900 it had become the trading center for a vast region and was the largest city between Salt Lake City and Portland."

Justifiably proud of their intriguing history, Baker City residents today strive to keep the community's heritage alive, a fact that is evident when you walk through the old downtown district, which is anchored by the beautifully renovated Geiser Grand Hotel. Celebrating the city's tangible connection to the Old West, the annual Miner's Jubilee is a three-day extravaganza that features an incredible array of activities for all ages. The festivities, which vary a bit each year and are announced on the Jubilee website, begin Friday morning, and include traditional blacksmithing and mining demonstrations at the Baker Heritage Museum (2480 Grove Street), an annual book sale at the Baker County Library (2400 Resort Street), sidewalk sales all along Main Street, and vendors offering all kinds of foods, products, and curiosities in Geiser Pollman Park, which is the hub of Jubilee activities and within easy walking distance of the museum, library, and Main Street. At midday the Paint Your Wagon film festival begins at the museum, and live music begins in the park, where festival attendees can try their hand at gold panning and a variety of other family-friendly activities.

Saturday action kicks off at 7 am with a Lions Club Breakfast in the park, the annual two-man golf scramble tournament at Quail Ridge Golf Course, and the Baker High School Miner's Jubilee 5K fun run/walk and 10K race. The colorful and popular Miner's Jubilee Parade begins at 10 am Saturday, while the film fest, live music, and park activities continue throughout the day. Saturday also delivers some of the most popular and unique Miner's Jubilee festivities: the Oregon State Gold Panning Championships, hosted by the Eastern Oregon Mining Association, offers divisions for kids, amateurs, and professionals; and the annual Miner's Jubilee Duck Races, with both adult and kid divisions, are held on the Powder River in the park and attended by substantial hilarity. During the evenings, Main Street is closed to vehicle traffic, and musicians take center stage under the gorgeous summer skies of Downtown Baker City, while a short walk away, the Baker County Fairgrounds host the Baker City Bronc and Bull Riding competitions, featuring top professional riders from throughout the region. With an onsite beer gardens, the rodeo grounds festivities continue late into the night both Saturday and Sunday.

Miner's Jubilee is one of the biggest, most entertaining, most family-friendly festivals in all of Eastern Oregon, and it draws tremendous crowds yet hardly ever seems crowded. A congenial atmosphere prevails, and attendees of all ages enjoy this citywide celebration immensely. In fact, Miner's Jubilee is so popular that it has become the host of many Baker High School class reunions; each year several of the school's classes organize their reunions to coincide with Jubilee. This community of about 10,000 people swells well beyond that total for jubilee, so visitors coming from afar should book lodging well in advance (for information about lodging and all other visitor-related topics, visit www.visitbaker.com and www.basecampbaker.com).

NEWBERRY EVENT MUSIC AND ARTS FESTIVAL TO DEFEAT MS

Between Sunriver and La Pine
DiamondStone Guest Lodges, 16693 Sprague Loop
Late July
www.newberryevent.com

Launched in 2013, the Newberry Event Music and Art Festival to Defeat MS gathers an impressive lineup of outstanding musicians to a beautiful outdoors venue near Sunriver—and all for a great cause—to help fight

Multiple Sclerosis (MS), a mysterious neurological and autoimmune disease that damages brain and spinal cord nerve cells. Chronic, and typically progressive, the disease produces symptoms that may include numbness, speech impairment, blurred vision, severe fatigue, and disabled muscular coordination. It can keep people from moving. Gloria

Proceeds from Newberry Event Music and Arts Festival help in the fight against Multiple Sclerosis.

Watt has battled MS for more than thirty years, but she and her husband, Doug, say, "When life gives you lemons, make lemonade!"

So with the help of many Central Oregon business sponsors and volunteers, they created the nonprofit Newberry Event Music and Arts Festival specifically to raise awareness and research funds for this thus-far incurable disease. Net proceeds benefit the Oregon National Multiple Sclerosis Society. They've garnered great acclaim and a loyal following for this fantastic limited-attendance event that feels like a big private party.

Held on beautiful rural acreage, the festival features nearly two dozen live music acts, with some of the best talent from the Northwest and beyond, representing myriad genres—rock, blues, reggae, jazz, folk, and more. Music plays from 10 am to 10 pm on two stages. The family-friendly event (kids under 12 get in free), has a country-fair atmosphere with many Pacific Northwest vendors selling a variety of handcrafted works. A silent auction of these products, plus sales from the great food vendors, local craft beers, Kombucha, distillery, and wine tasting, all help raise money for the cause. Over the years, the Newberry Event has featured such notable acts as Fishbone, Craig Chaquico, Riders in the Sky, and Lukas Nelson & Promise of the Real. Buy tickets for the festival—and make a charitable donation—via the event website.

Tent camping in open fields or shady pines is free and encouraged so you don't miss a thing. Limited RV sites are available. So if you're looking to have a great time for a great cause, join the loving Newberry Event community: Multiple Sclerosis keeps people from moving; come rock out and dance for those who can't.

NORTH POWDER HUCKLEBERRY FESTIVAL

North Powder
2nd Street and Old Oregon Trail
Last Saturday in July
www.unioncountychamber.org/item/north-powder-huckleberry-festival

In celebration of wild huckleberries, which grow profusely high in the surrounding Wallowa and Elkhorn Mountains, the tiny far-eastern community of North Powder annually throws this summertime bash that offers something for everyone. The North Powder Huckleberry Festival gets underway with a community breakfast and all-classes school reunion beginning at 7 am, followed by the Huckleberry Festival Parade at 11.

Meanwhile, at 8 am the starting gun sounds for the popular Huckleberry Hustle 5K and 10K fun run/walk, and the Huckleberry Hot Rod Show & Shine begins, with automobile enthusiasts rolling out a bedazzling assortment of beautifully restored classic cars. The city park hosts live entertainment throughout the day, including regional bands. The lineup of activities changes slightly year to year, and for a time the festival hosted a popular and raucous mud volleyball tournament, and may offer something similar in the future (perhaps sand volleyball).

During the afternoon, the kids' activities get underway (including a

Vintage automobiles line the streets of North Powder during the Huckleberry Festival.

Dragon Theater Puppet Show), and the huckleberry dessert contest judging begins—and in case you're drooling in jealousy, wishing you were among the huckleberry dessert judges, worry not: festival attendees can try various huckleberry delights available from food vendors, and in the evening the local fire station hosts a benefit BBQ and huckleberry dessert contest auction. Craft (and food) vendors are available all day, followed by the North Powder Rural Fire Department BBQ dinner, and finally the popular festival nightcap, the annual street dance featuring live music. Attendees interested in participating in the fun run and volleyball tournament (if it is revived) should register early.

High in the nearby mountains, wild huckleberries are coming into season in late summer, so the festival makes a great highlight to a weekend of exploring the Elkhorn Range just a short drive west from North Powder. Consult the Wallowa-Whitman National Forest for access information and other details.

WE LIKE 'EM SHORT FILM FESTIVAL

Baker City
Eltrym Theater, 1809 1st Street
Mid-August
www.welikeemshort.com

At first blush it may seem incongruous that the small far-eastern community of Baker City would spawn an award-winning film festival, but upon further examination such surprise is short lived for Baker City, today home to the historic Eltrym Theater, was an early proponent of the performing arts. By 1884 the Oregon Short Line Railroad arrived in Baker City, and by 1900 this scenic community with the commanding views of the Elkhorn Range was the largest city on the rail line between Salt Lake City and Portland. Money—from mining and ranching and other pursuits—flowed freely, engendering an upper class eager to embrace the finer appointments, such as theater. Likely its first performance stage was the Rust Opera House, opened in the late 1800s; the city enjoyed nearly continuous service by various theaters and entrepreneurs whose interests included the performing arts.

The modern-day incarnation of these visionaries is multifaceted artist and former New Yorker Brian Vegter, now a Baker City resident, who created the We Like 'Em Short Film Festival (WLES) in 2009 to celebrate the art of animated and comedic short films, providing a platform for independent filmmakers from around the world to share their talent and projects. Short films present a challenge for scriptwriters, animators, and filmmakers, requiring concise and creative storytelling that captivates an audience quickly and holds it raptly. Annually WLES screens a variety of outstanding short films, all twenty minutes or less, and showcases local and regional filmmakers as well as films from around the world. Each year WLES hosts talented directors, with past special visitors including Chel White, Doug Lussenhop, Benjamin Morgan, and Joanna Priestley. Directors conduct workshops and presentations during this four-day festival and even work with the Baker High School Film Arts Club, one of the beneficiaries of proceeds from the event.

All short films—more than fifty each year—are shown on Eltrym Theater's giant #1 screen through a Christie Digital Projector. Because they are so short, these films are generally only seen at film festivals and on the internet, so WLES provides big-screen showings that allow audiences to appreciate the vision and creativity of these projects. In 2014, WLES was honored with an Ovation Award from the Oregon Festival and Events Association, which recognized the festival as the Best Fine Art or Performing Arts Festival in Oregon.

Such prestige is further bolstered by the wonderful host city: Baker City exudes Old West charm and small-town congeniality; it's a terrific place to spend a few days, not only to take in the festival but to sample the community's variety of fine restaurants, fun pubs, and interesting shops, and to branch out to explore the verdant forested mountains nearby and their many hidden treasures. During the evenings of the festival, a variety of venues in the core downtown area host live music—and few towns in Oregon are more pleasant for a summer-evening stroll than historic Baker City. Tickets for WLES (modestly priced) are available via the event website, and for filmmakers aspiring to have their work showcased at this ever-expanding film fest, heed Vegter's instructions: "Be creative, make us laugh and keep it short."

The historic Eltrym Theatre anchors the award-winning We Like 'Em Short Film Festival.

EASTERN OREGON BEER FESTIVAL

La Grande
Union County Fairgrounds
June
www.eobeerfest.org

La Grande is a wonderful little city, a place where academia meets agrarianism, an historic community occupying a bucolic valley hemmed in by the Blue Mountains rising above town and the majestic Wallowa Mountains to the east. The downtown area, walkable, offers an alluring assemblage of restaurants and shops; at eateries like 10 Depot Street, ranchers comingle with college students from Eastern Oregon University.

It's the perfect town for a summer brew fest, hence the Eastern Oregon Beer Festival, a spritely bash hosted by La Grande Main Street Downtown, which earmarks proceeds from the festival for community and business development, community events, and beautification projects. In recent years, the Eastern Oregon Beer Festival has attracted some thirty breweries from Eastern Oregon and beyond, including a number of eastside breweries whose ales are rarely seen beyond their host communities. Throughout the day, regional musicians entertain the crowd; a variety of food vendors make sure no one goes hungry; and local and regional artisans peddle unique wares. This one-day event falls on a Saturday, so the ideal strategy is to arrive in La Grande on Friday and explore the town's spirited little downtown area: strike up a conversation with the locals and ask their advice for the best places for a drink or a meal.

The festival runs from noon to 8 pm, with an after-party event from 8 pm to 10 pm, which costs a nominal entrance fee. Attendees can buy general admission passes or VIP passes, which provide exclusive tastings, early admission, and other perks; all paid attendees receive a commemorative glass tasting mug. However, passes to

Choose your favorite ale at the outdoor Eastern Oregon Beer Festival in La Grande.

the event are not available at the gate (unless the event does not sell out in advance); general admission passes are available at a few local and regional businesses, but attendees coming from afar should buy them online at the festival website. VIP passes are available online only. The festival organizers decided that advance purchase of a limited number of passes would ensure the best possible experience for beer lovers, many of whom come from distant points. And they were right—lines are minimal, the atmosphere is relaxed, and the attending breweries rarely run out of beer. Nondrinking admission is $5 at the gate. Hotel and motel space in La Grande is somewhat limited, so book early; the festival has also arranged campground lodging onsite (see festival website).

PACIFIC CREST TRAIL DAYS (AKA PCT DAYS)

Cascade Locks
Marine Park, 355 Wa Na Pa Street
Mid-August
www.pctdays.com

Stretching for 2,659 miles from the Mexican border to the Canadian border, through the Sierra Nevada and Cascade Mountains, the Pacific Crest Trail was completed in 1993, with many of its segments leading through designated wilderness areas in California, Oregon, and Washington, not to mention six national parks. Along its colossal course, the PCT (as devotees lovingly call it) necessarily intersects highways, backroads, and rivers; it crosses some sixty major mountain passes and dips though nineteen major canyons. But only once does it run into a truly monumental obstacle: the mighty Columbia River. The PCT meets the Columbia at

Outdoors enthusiast check out the vendors at Pacific Crest Trail Days.

Cascade Locks and crosses the river on the 1,856-foot-long Bridge of the Gods a few miles downstream from Bonneville Dam.

The bridge is, of course, an essential link in the Pacific Crest Trail and the perfect place to gather in honor of the PCT and everything wilderness represents to the American collective consciousness. So each August, Pacific Crest Trail Days, a three-day festival at Cascade Locks, draws throngs of likeminded outdoor enthusiasts together for an energetic celebration of hiking, camping, backpacking, and other pursuits. Attendees learn about essential skills and get the scoop on the latest outdoor products from a variety of exhibiting sponsors, including some of the biggest names in outdoor recreation alongside innovative small companies. Moreover, PCT Days includes all kinds of fun activities, games, and presentations, along with outstanding local food and beverage vendors, live music, and great deals at the largest gear expo in the country.

With tent-camping available for a modest fee on Thunder Island or by vehicle at the Cascade Locks Marine Park, many attendees stay for the entire event, but day-trippers are equally welcome, and the festival even serves as a special respite for hikers navigating the PCT. Festivities kick off Friday afternoon with the opening of the gear expo (which continues all day Saturday) and with the rollicking evening PCT Days Welcome Party featuring games, trivia, food, drinks, and more, followed by live music (each summer, the event website announces all the activities and details for PCT Days). Saturday delivers a full slate of fun activities and games, with live music capping off the evening—if you're visiting PCT Days for one day, Saturday it should be. Throughout the day, attendees can buy inexpensive raffle tickets at the PCT Days info booth, and then come evening hope to win great gear prizes in the jubilant PCT Days Gear Raffle at the big stage. All proceeds from raffle ticket sales go to the Pacific Crest Trail Association and the American Long Distance Hiking Association-West.

The final special event occurs Sunday morning, when PCT Days treats Pacific Crest Trail thru-hikers to a free breakfast before they shoulder their packs and hit the trail. PCT Days is the perfect way to bone up on outdoor skills, check out all the latest gear, mingle with outdoor-loving friends old and new, and revel in the words of Edward Abbey: "Wilderness is not a luxury but a necessity of the human spirit."

BEND BREWFEST

Bend
Les Schwab Amphitheater, Old Mill District
Mid-August
https://bendbrewfest.com

These days, beerocratic Bend doesn't do much of anything that isn't a lively major production, and millennials might be surprised to learn that not long before they were born, busy, bustling, ebullient Bend was a rather quiet little oasis where strangers said hello when passing on the quiet downtown sidewalks. Such nostalgia aside, these days Bend is a swank destination drawing visitors from all quarters; it is now the state's fifth-largest metropolitan areas and among the fastest growing in the nation.

Bend is also one of the most beercentric cities in the West, as evidenced not only by its myriad always-crowded breweries but also by the massive, jovial, frolicking Bend Brewfest, spanning three days each August at the sprawling lawn of the Les Schwab Amphitheater in the Old Mill District just south of downtown. Shoulder-to-shoulder crowds vie for samples of dozens upon dozens of regional beers in this incredible event that surely must by now rank among the most grandiose brew festivals in the state. In recent years, the Bend Brewfest has boasted at least 100 breweries, cideries, and wineries, and that number may soon hit 200. One of the popular aspects of the Bend Brewfest are the XTap samplings at the Brewtality Tent: numerous participating brewers bring low-production specialty beers to sample during designated time slots and the brewers themselves are on hand at the

Bend Brewfest is a massive, three-day celebration of regional ales.

Brewtality Tent to talk about their creations. The Brewfest begins on Thursday at noon and runs through Saturday, open until 11 each night. Thursday generally begins rather inauspiciously, making it a great time to find nearby parking—get there early and plan to stay into the night. There is no actual admission fee, but sampling requires one-time purchase of a souvenir mug that comes with five tasting tokens and additional tokens are sold separately.

A variety of excellent food vendors (cash only/ATM onsite) provide an eclectic lineup of meals and snacks. Parents are welcome to bring children up until 5 pm; thereafter the event is 21 and over only. August in Bend almost always means all-day intense sunshine, so bring sunscreen, sunglasses, and perhaps even a low-profile carryable beach/camp chair. Parking is always a challenge, so consult the event parking map at www.bendconcerts. com/parking_map.html. Lodging in Bend is even more challenging than parking, so make hotel reservations weeks if not months in advance. Campgrounds are scattered throughout the region, including ever-popular and conveniently located Tumalo State Park on the north end of town. This three-day festival allows readmission, so you only need to buy the required sampling mug on your first entry; spend some time exploring the city, then come back for more frivolity at one of Oregon's biggest brew fests.

PAINTED HILLS FESTIVAL

Mitchell
Dowtown area
Saturday of Labor Day weekend
www.mitchelloregon.us/about-mitchell/painted-hills-festival/

Oregon's Painted Hills, aptly named for their kaleidoscopic mix of geological layers, are part of the John Day Fossil Beds National Monument and located northwest of the tiny, peaceful town of Mitchell in Wheeler County. The Painted Hills display layered bedrock in bands of different colors corresponding to different geological eras, and to the delight of photographers, often put on a bedazzling display as the sun cracks the horizon on a summer morning. The perfect time to visit the Painted Hills and the nearby John Day Fossil Beds is Labor Day weekend, when you'll have plenty of time not only to take in the natural wonders but also attend the fun-filled Painted Hills Festival in Mitchell.

Launched in 1995, this jovial festival offers not only a little something for just about everyone but also a glimpse into the Eastern Oregon small-town pride that justifiably permeates this close-knit community. The locals—there are less than 200 of them—embrace visitors and eagerly share information about this beautifully rugged part of the state. The Painted Hills Festival begins with a series of fun runs—a half marathon,

The Old West on display at the Painted Hills Festival in Mitchell.

10K, and 5K—first thing Saturday morning. The half marathon begins at the picnic area ("Painted Hills Park") at the Painted Hills nine miles from town, and the shorter races begin along the half-marathon route so that all three events end at the finish line in Mitchell. A shuttle bus is available to deliver runners to the starting lines. After the races, an awards ceremony is held at the city park in Mitchell and runners can use the showers at the Mitchell School.

By the time the races end, the weather typically begins to heat up, and the Painted Hills Festival activities in town kick into high gear, beginning with a parade down Main Street featuring horse riders, vintage autos, motorcycles, pioneer-era wagons, fire trucks, the Red Hat Society ladies, and more. Next come the festival games. Can you devour watermelon at an alarming rate? Then test your limits by entering the popular watermelon-eating contest; or take the kids to the children's games area, and check out the quilt show and raffle. Throughout the day, vendors fill the city park, offering an eclectic variety of goods, including plenty of food options, and live music entertains the crowds, culminating with a street dance in the evening.

The Painted Hills Festival perfectly captures the small-town America spirit, celebrating the local culture and proudly presenting it to welcomed guests from afar.

JUNIPER JAM

Enterprise
Wallowa County Fairgrounds
Saturday of Labor Day weekend
www.juniperjam.com

If you dig music and love remote wonders, Juniper Jam in Enterprise is a must-do event—it truly is the sweetest little music festival in Eastern Oregon, as the organizers bill this one-day party. In fact, considering the gorgeous venue—the high ramparts of the Wallowa Mountains looming as a splendid backdrop—Juniper Jam is one of the sweetest music festivals in the entire state.

Juniper Jam annually delivers a superb lineup of professional musicians. Genres run the gamut: rock, Americana, blues, bluegrass, folk, acoustic, country, swing, jazz, R&B, and more—and plenty of musicians brilliantly blur the lines between genres. The festival kicks off at noon, with the first musicians taking the stage at 1 pm; the music then continues until nearly 11 pm. Food vendors provide an array of excellent options, including beer and wine, and local artisans demonstrate their talents and offer their art for sale. The festival also includes the TR Ritchie Memorial Songwriting Contest. TR Ritchie (1946–2014) was a beloved member of the songwriting community around the country, with deep ties to the Northwest. To honor his life's work in music, writing, poetry, and art, songwriters are invited to enter their best recent work to win a showcase spot at Juniper Jam, along with cash prizes.

Few music festivals can match the high-mountain majesty of Juniper Jam in Enterprise.

Tickets to Juniper Jam, which are inexpensive, are available in advance online, and buying ahead of time is a good idea in case the event sells out.

Enterprise is a long ways from everywhere, so if you attend the Juniper Jam, plan to stay for the weekend and make lodging arrangements well in advance (for a list of options, consult the Wallowa County Chamber of Commerce, www.wallowacountychamber.com). In addition to motels, hotels, and B&Bs, the area has several campgrounds. This beautiful valley and surrounding mountains offer many diversions: drive to the rim of Hells Canyon or down into the Imnaha River canyon; hike the trails of the Eagle Cap Wilderness; fish or play at scenic Wallowa Lake; visit the many art galleries and eclectic shops in Enterprise and Joseph; sample the restaurants, pubs, and bars in both communities (hopheads won't want to miss a visit to Terminal Gravity Brewery in Enterprise). And that's just the tip of the iceberg in a faraway corner of Oregon brimming with options for outdoors enthusiasts.

SISTERS FOLK FESTIVAL

Sisters
Village Green Park and other venues
September weekend after Labor Day
www.sistersfolkfestival.org

From humble beginnings in 1995, the Sisters Folk Festival, held each September, now attracts throngs of music lovers to Oregon's favorite mountain town just thirty minutes northwest of Bend. This joyous celebration of roots music, from blues to bluegrass, takes over the town for three days and delivers a star-studded lineup of world-class musicians.

Among the dozens upon dozens of artists performing in Sisters over the years have been such notables as Ian Tyson, Natalie MacMaster, Jesse Winchester, Chris Smither, Dave Carter, John Gorka, Cheryl Wheeler, Ruthie Foster, The Subdudes, The Waifs, Tim O'Brien, The Wailin' Jennys, Jon Cleary, Frank Solivan & Dirty Kitchen, Lake Street Dive, Anais Mitchell, Shakey Graves, Eric Bibb, Richard Thompson, and Shawn Mullins. Each year's lineup is announced by springtime and tickets to the event sell out soon thereafter.

The three-day-pass tickets ($150 for adults/$50 for youth in recent years) are available through the event website, and a perusal of the lineup in recent years certainly underscores the need to buy tickets early: these days the

Sisters Folk Festival delivers a star-studded lineup of musicians to several venues throughout town.

Sisters Folk Festival annually hosts about forty nationally acclaimed artists performing an eclectic mix of music at eleven different venues throughout this ponderosa-studded community of 2,500 people. The venues range from the 1,100-seat Sisters Art Works tent and 900-seat Village Green Park stage to intimate quarters such as the Belfry, Depot Café, and Angeline's Bakery.

The entire town is foot-traffic friendly and all the music venues are within easy walking distance from one another, and whatever path you take from concert to concert is sure to lead past any number of wonderful restaurants, bars, and shops for which Sisters is known—this beautiful little town knows how to treat visitors. Parking is available near all the venues and all parking in Sisters is free. Be warned, however, that lodging options fill up early and fully for the Sisters Folk Festival, so make plans well in advance if you want a hotel, motel, or B&B for the weekend (consult the Sisters Chamber of Commerce for lodging options and other visitor information, www.sisterscountry.com).

HOOD RIVER HOPS FEST

Hood River
Columbia Lot, 5th and Columbia
Late September
www.hoodriver.org/hops-fest/

A low-key street-party atmosphere with live music from some of the hottest bands from Portland and the Columbia Gorge; food vendors serving up a great mix of eats; and best of all, more than fifty breweries pouring more than sixty flavor-packed fresh-hop beers in one of Oregon's hippest most happening small towns: no wonder the Hood River Hops Fest garnered a silver medal for best beer festival from the *Willamette Week* Oregon Beer Awards amid brutally stiff competition in a state burgeoning with beer fests.

Since 2003, this energetic brew festival has gathered world-class fresh-hopped brews by the dozens, not only from the myriad breweries in and near the Gorge but from throughout Oregon and even a few from Washington and California, and ranging from the best-known giants in the industry to small-batch nano breweries. Even the most ardent hophead is likely to find a brewery or two he or she has never before encountered, and the flavor profiles within the fresh-hops genre are surprisingly broad, assuring every beer lover will find something awesome.

While the vast majority of beers are made with dried hops, fresh-hop beers take advantage of the more floral taste and aromas of green, freshly picked hop cones to brew special seasonal ales. It's a run-and-gun style of brewing, reputedly pioneered here in the Pacific Northwest where most American hops are grown—the hops need to go from vine to brewery very quickly and into the beer speedily as well. These autumn specialties don't age well, so the season for them is fleeting, but their flavor profiles are so expressive that Northwest beer aficionados flock to breweries producing fresh-hop beers and to the handful of festivals dedicated to these brews.

The Hood River Hops Fest occurs downtown at the Columbia Lot at 5th and Columbia—right across the street from Full Sale Brewing and a short block away from Double Mountain Brewery—and runs from noon until 8 pm, with live music ongoing throughout the event. Tickets are available for purchase in advance via the event website and also at the gate, with the beer garden ticket package including entry, a commemorative glass, and five tasting

Tokens and mug at the ready for Hood River Hops Fest.

tokens; additional tokens are available for purchase at the festival. Only those 21 and over can drink beer, but until 5 pm attendees under age 21 are welcome and get in for free (and a special kids area has games and activities for children); after 5 pm, the festival is 21-and-over only. Entry lines can get rather lengthy but move rapidly, so arriving early is a wise tactic. The Hood River Chamber of Commerce, www.hoodriver.org, creates special Hops Fest accommodation packages and can provide ample information on lodging and activities in the area.

OREGON'S ALPENFEST

Wallowa Valley
Enterprise, Joseph, and Wallowa Lake
Last weekend in September
www.oregonalpenfest.blogspot.com

The only Swiss-Bavarian festival in the Western United States, Oregon's Alpenfest is a joyous, lively, and colorful celebration of the unique cultures of the Alps, and the beautiful mountain towns of Joseph and Enterprise serve perfectly for such a festival. Occupying a verdant, bucolic highland valley at the foot of the snow-capped ramparts of the rugged Wallowa Mountains in Northeast Oregon, these sun-drenched communities and the surrounding region comprise what is aptly nicknamed "Oregon's Little Switzerland."

This weekend-long family-oriented event features ongoing performances by talented musicians and dancers who come to Oregon's Alpenfest from near and far. Attendees marvel at the amazing alphorns—traditional wooden horns, first used hundreds of years ago, that range from ten to more than thirteen feet long. These conically bored hollow tubes are made from wood strips, usually spruce, and bound with birch bark or cane. Accordion players also mesmerize the crowds; alpine bands, renowned yodelers, and remarkably adept folk dancers recall the grandest performing traditions of the cultures emanating from Europe's most prominent mountains.

Oregon's Alpenfest kicks off on Thursday afternoon in Downtown Enterprise with the Main Street Procession and Opening Ceremony— the first of numerous opportunities to enjoy the alphorn specialists, accordionists, and master Swiss yodelers. Right afterward, events move to Terminal Gravity Brewery—the award-winning craft ale producer that opened its doors in Enterprise in 1997—for the ceremonial tapping of the first keg of Terminal Gravity Alpenfest beer, with tastes offered for a modest donation and full glasses and meals also available.

Friday ushers in activities and performances at the de facto festival headquarters, the rustic, historic Edelweiss Inn at Wallowa Lake, just outside of Joseph, beginning with the Alpine Breakfast (8 am to noon). The Alpine Fair—featuring art, craft, and food vendors—begins at noon outside the inn and continues into early evening, running all three days of the weekend. The fair not only highlights many local artisans selling their wares but also features artisan-made bratwurst and sauerkraut, plus wine and beer. Inside the Edelweiss Inn, the Alpenshow begins midday and runs into the night Friday and Saturday, presenting a litany of performances from dancers, yodelers, and musicians—including alphornists—all bedecked in traditional costume. In case you need to brush up on your polka and waltz steps, free lessons are offered by championship polka dancers twice a day. A highlight of the Alpenshow is the full bratwurst meal, served up at a modest price in addition to the entry fee to the show. Alluring Downtown Joseph, with its myriad galleries, restaurants, and shops, also hosts visiting accordionists on Main Street.

Oregon's Alpenfest is unique—while Oktoberfest celebrations are held at numerous venues throughout Oregon and the Northwest, there's only one Alpenfest, and the venue couldn't be more inspiring—especially for visitors lucky enough to find the high crags of the Wallowas dusted with autumn's first snow.

The dance hall comes alive with color and motion during Oregon's Alpenfest.

SISTERS FRESH HOP FESTIVAL

Sisters
Three Creeks Brewing Facility,
   265 East Barclay Drive
Early October
www.sistersfreshhopfest.com

Central Oregon seems to spawn another new craft brewery about once a month, and while that's an exaggeration, the region is home to some of the best and most popular ale producers in the Northwest. The Sisters Fresh Hop Festival, started in 2010, brings a bunch of them together in one great location at exactly the right time: when the hops are harvested. This convivial and pleasantly low-key festival focuses on flavor-packed fresh-hopped beers—in the words of F. Florian Klemp, "Supplied with fresh-picked hops, brewers fire their kettle to capture the hop in its most natural state. The jaunt from field to wort is harried, lest the precious and essential components lose their verdant charm, as Mother Nature waits for no brewer. Wet hop ales are both earthly and ethereal, and composed to flaunt their delicate, juicy character."

Moreover, fall is idyllic in Sisters. This forested little mountain town, population 2,500, buzzes with tourists from Memorial Day to Labor Day, but quiets considerably come autumn—the perfect time for a brew fest. This annual event held at the Three Creeks Brewing Facility also features breweries from other parts of Oregon, bringing the total up to about two dozen beer makers, assuring that attendees can find something they like. Unlike big-city beer festivals in the Northwest, the Sisters Fresh Hop Festival tends to be up close and personal: you won't need to wait in long lines to get a sample or a pint, and many of the brewers themselves are on hand, eager to talk about their latest fresh-hop experiments. Festival attendees pay a small fee for a pint

Sisters Fresh Hop Festival features beers brewed with fresh-picked, rather than dried, hops.

glass and $1 tokens are worth a four-ounce sample from any brewery.

This is a family-friendly event (children can attend with their parents; 21 and over to drink); the venue is within walking distance of the many unique shops and fun restaurants in Sisters, and the town offers a variety of lodging options, including nearby campgrounds, one of which—Sisters Creekside Campground—is in town, just a fifteen-minute walk south from the brew fest (handy if you've waded through samples from two dozen breweries) and not far from festival-sponsor Three Creeks Brewery's pub (handy if you didn't quite sate your palate at the festival). One thing about Sisters, however: even after the prime summer tourism season, the town's hotel/motel rooms often sell out on weekends, so make reservations well ahead of time.

KLAMATH BASIN POTATO FESTIVAL

Merrill
Merrill Park Civic Center, 365 W Front Street
Mid-October
www.klamathbasinpotatofestival.com

Celebrating one of the Klamath Basin's most important agricultural products, the Klamath Basin Potato Festival, despite a history dating back to 1934, remains an under-the-radar, fun-filled festival that annually draws upwards of 2,000 people—twice the population of its host town, Merrill, located about twenty miles southeast of Klamath Falls, near the California border. Little known outside the Klamath Basin, the potato festival is classic Americana, a celebration of agriculture, community cohesiveness, and small-town values. The few outsiders who travel from afar to indulge in this unique festival are treated like old friends. In fact, far removed from Oregon's population centers, Merrill is a friendly agrarian community that embraces the crowds that gather for this weekend-long event.

One of the highlights of the festival is the free barbequed beef and baked potato feast served up beginning in the early afternoon outside the Merrill Civic Center, which is the hub of activities for the event. Meanwhile, the Civic Center Field hosts all-day Pop Warner football games on Saturday, and a five-mile fun run—the Linkville Lopers Spud Run—begins Saturday morning. Midday on Saturday, the Potato Festival Parade courses through Downtown Merrill and, among other participants, features each year's grand marshal, as well as the

Potato Festival Court and its queen, chosen at Lost River High School during the week leading up to the extravaganza.

The Klamath Basin Potato Festival is extensively family friendly, but adults can enjoy live music and a beer gardens. Central to the entire weekend festival is the

Local agriculture meets local arts and crafts at the Klamath Basin Potato Festival.

exhibit and vendor hall, which opens Friday at the civic center, featuring a variety of displays such as the biggest, strangest, and most uniform potatoes as well as other produce. Food and produce contests allow all entrants and include many different categories for food, including, of course, potato dishes and products, as well as myriad categories for commercially grown potatoes; craft contests include categories for virtually any art medium, as well as pumpkin carving and scarecrow making. Vendors offer food, produce, arts and crafts, and more.

Lodging is limited in Merrill. The town offers two hotels and an RV park, but make reservations well ahead of time for festival weekend. Otherwise, reserve a room in Klamath Falls. Merrill also has several small restaurants, all of which are good, and patronizing them is part of the experience of enjoying this pleasant, quiet little community.

EASTERN OREGON FILM FESTIVAL

La Grande
Various venues
Late October
www.eofilmfest.com

One of Eastern Oregon's most intriguing communities, La Grande seamlessly melds what might seem disparate cultures—old-fashioned Western Americana, based on rural ranching, forestry, and mining, and the academia that comes with an institution of higher learning, in this case, Eastern Oregon University (EOU). The town captures the essence of both cultures, and sitting at dinner at 10 Depot Street, or sipping a drink in Benchwarmers, or enjoying breakfast at the Long

Branch, you're likely to see timber workers sharing stories with students, ranchers conversing easily with academicians, farmers chatting with artists.

That community spirit, that melding of cultures, is what makes La Grande such an ideal host community for the Eastern Oregon Film Festival (EOFF), which annually screens a carefully selected eclectic mix of outstanding films at several different venues around town, including EOU, the Granada Theater (built in 1927), and the stately old Stage Door Theater, opened in 1910 as the Liberty Theater and now on the National Register of Historic Places. Each year EOFF presents more than thirty films, showcasing works produced by some of the best independent filmmakers in the business, and giving voice to both established veterans and innovative newcomers. Each year, the festival invites a number of the filmmakers to attend in person, providing film fans a chance to converse with them.

In addition to the films themselves, EOFF engenders a joyous, festive atmosphere with three evening after-party events held at the festival's center of activities, HQ at 112 Depot Street, downtown. The after-parties feature outstanding, energetic live music performed by a cadre of local and regional bands, along with drinks and appetizers, and the town's cozy downtown area transforms into a lively congenial scene. The festival officially opens Thursday morning when attendees can pick up movie passes at HQ, and screenings begin that evening and pick up again Friday morning; Friday and Saturday, films run all day, with HQ opening at 10 am and films running from late morning until the final show times around 7 pm.

Eastern Oregon Film Festival delivers a great lineup of carefully chosen films to audiences in La Grande.

A nonprofit enterprise, EOFF relies on support from the public, and one great way to help the effort and reap benefits is to become a member of the festival, which offers several different sponsorship buy-in levels. Members enjoy guaranteed admission to all screenings, music performances, and special events, and get priority seating for all the films, get their names in the official festival program, have access to the EOFF library of independent movies, and even get access to festival video equipment packages for use with independent movie making in Eastern Oregon. Members also receive various discounts and invites to events throughout the year.

In 2017, EOFF captured widespread acclaim when it was selected by *Movie Maker* magazine as one the "25 coolest film festivals in the world." The editors noted that "…the tiny city of La Grande has quietly fostered a handcrafted festival that delivers quality and a wide-open sensibility without much hubbub."

Maybe not, but EOFF certainly exudes enough hubbub to make it well worth the drive to one of Eastern Oregon's coolest little towns.

KLAMATH SNOWFLAKE FESTIVAL

Klamath Falls
Various venues
Late November to early December
www.klamathsnowflake.com

Oregon's largest winter celebration, the Klamath Snowflake Festival kicks off the Christmas season as a sixteen-day multievent extravaganza with something for everyone. The most highly attended event is the Snowflake Parade on Main Street in downtown, held on the last Thursday of the festival after dark to fully bedazzle onlookers with colorfully lit floats, trucks, and other vehicles.

Kicking off the parade is the ever-popular Snowflake Mile, a fun run down Main Street for runners of all ability levels, many of whom dress up in holiday attire. Some years, parade onlookers enjoy pleasant weather with temperatures in the 40s, while other years, bitter cold sets in, and sometimes falling snow provides a wonderful wintery ambiance. Naturally, parade attendees should dress warmly, and when the festivities end, perhaps seek refuge from the cold in one of downtown's fun restaurants or bars.

The Snowflake Parade draws its audience from throughout Southern Oregon and beyond, and while many of the other festival activities—Gingerbread House Competition, Bowl with Santa, Snowflake Dance, Santa Freeze, just to name a few—are mostly attended by local and area residents, the festival also offers the Ugly Sweater 5K Run, exactly the kind of eclectic road race that appeals to dedicated fun runners everywhere (preregistration is required).

The Klamath Snowflake Festival begins with the afternoon arrival of Santa Claus at Kiger Stadium, and thereafter, over the course of two weeks, children have a dozen or so opportunities to meet Santa; a full list of Santa appearances and festival events is available on the festival website.

Klamath Falls—130 miles south of Bend and 70 miles over the Cascades from the Ashland/Medford area—is a long drive for most Oregonians, so stay a while when you get there and immerse yourself in this friendly and engaging community. Among the worthwhile sights is the Favell Museum, which displays an incredible collection of Native American artifacts; the city also has a pair of under-the-radar breweries—Klamath Basin Brewery and Mia and Pia's Pizzeria & Brewhouse—and a small assemblage of excellent and oft-lively restaurants.

Runners stride through downtown Klamath Falls during the Snowflake Mile, a popular event at the Klamath Snowflake Festival.

FESTIVALS BY AREA

FESTIVALS BY CATEGORY

ACTIVITIES FESTIVALS

AGRICULTURAL/PRODUCE FESTIVALS

ART AND CRAFT FESTIVALS

BEER FESTIVALS

April
Nano Beer Fest *20*
May
The Little Woody Barrel-Aged Beer,
Cider & Whiskey Festival,
Medford *180*
June
Organic Beer Fest *36*
Rye Beer Fest *29*
Saké Fest PDX *35*
Oregon Garden Brewcamp *81*
Lakeside Brewfest *143*
Lake of the Woods Beer Fest *186*
Eastern Oregon Beer Festival *196*
July
Oregon Brewers Festival *43*
Portland Craft Beer Festival *37*
Roadhouse Brewfest *40*
August
Oakridge Keg & Cask Festival *93*
Lighthouse Brew Festival *152*
Dog Days of Summer Oregon Coast
Brew Festival *150*
Bend Brewfest *199*
September
Dogtoberfest *50*
Mount Angel Oktoberfest *99*
Pacific Northwest Brew Cup *157*
Lincoln City Chowder & Brewfest *161*
Gold Beach Brew & Art Festival *155*
The Little Woody Barrel-Aged Beer,
Cider & Whiskey Festival, Bend *180*
Hood River Hops Fest *204*
October
Killer Pumpkin Festival *56*
Sisters Fresh Hop Festival *208*
December
Holiday Ale Festival *60*

CAR FESTIVALS
August
Sutherlin Blackberry Festival *117*

CIDER FESTIVALS
March
Cider Rite of Spring *19*

April
Hood River Hard-Pressed Cider
Fest *172*
May
The Little Woody Barrel-Aged Beer,
Cider & Whiskey Festival,
Medford *180*
June
Cider Summit PDX *31*
September
The Little Woody Barrel-Aged Beer,
Cider & Whiskey Festival, Bend *180*

COMMUNITY FESTIVALS
February
Gorse Blossom Festival *127*
April
Northwest Cherry Festival *175*
May
Brookings Azalea Festival *141*
Oakridge Tree Planting Festival *73*
Florence Rhododendron Festival *139*
June
Portland Rose Festival *25*
Festival of Balloons *32*
Lebanon Strawberry Festival *79*
Clamboree & Glass Art Festival *146*
Watershed Festival *187*
July
North Powder Huckleberry Festival *193*
Miner's Jubilee *189*
August
Tualatin Crawfish Festival *45*
Homer Davenport Community
Festival *89*
Aumsville Corn Festival *94*
Sutherlin Blackberry Festival *117*
September
Carlton Crush Harvest Festival *96*

FOOD (SPECIALTY) FESTIVALS

January

Oregon Truffle Festival *65*

February

Newport Seafood & Wine Festival *129*

WurstFest *69*

March

Oregon Chocolate Festival *111*

Oregon Cheese Festival *112*

Savor Cannon Beach Wine & Culinary Festival *131*

April

Northwest Cherry Festival *175*

May

Lakeside Crawdad Festival *137*

June

Clamboree & Glass Art Festival *146*

Rhubarb Festival *183*

July

North Powder Huckleberry Festival *193*

August

Tualatin Crawfish Festival *45*

Oregon Honey (& Mead) Festival *116*

Sutherlin Blackberry Festival *117*

Blackberry Arts Festival *153*

September

Bandon Cranberry Festival *158*

Lincoln City Chowder & Brewfest *161*

Mill-Luck Salmon Celebration *154*

Southern Oregon Smoked Salmon Fest *121*

October

The Wedge *55*

Mushroom Festival *103*

Klamath Basin Potato Festival *209*

December

Mount Angel Hazelnut Fest & German Holiday Market *104*

HISTORICAL FESTIVALS

May

Sheep to Shawl *75*

July

Miner's Jubilee *189*

August

Homer Davenport Community Festival *89*

September

Molalla Apple Festival *97*

LITERARY FESTIVALS

November

Portland Book Festival *58*

MUSIC FESTIVALS

February

Sabertooth Psychedelic Stoner Rock Micro Fest *12*

April

Birding & Blues Festival *133*

May

Wildflower & Music Festival *78*

Ashland World Music Festival *114*

June

Britt Music & Arts Festival *115*

4 Peaks Music Festival *184*

Wheeler County Bluegrass Festival *188*

July

Waterfront Blues Festival *38*

Wildwood MusicFest and Campout *86*

Newberry Event Music and Arts Festival to Defeat MS *191*

September

Sisters Folk Festival *203*

Juniper Jam *202*

PHOTOGRAPHY CREDITS

Page 8-9, 62-63, 106-107, 124-125, 164-165, 221: Ashland Chamber of Commerce. **11:** Jean Heffernan Fleming. **12-13, 16-17, 40, 77, 152, 168-169:** McMenamins/ Kathleen Nyberg, photographer. **14:** Northwest Film Center. **15–16:** Dan Malech. **18, 50-51:** Lucky Labrador Brew Pub, Ltd. **19:** Northwest Cider Association, Sherrye Wyatt. **20:** Brandon Mikel. **21:** Sven Bonnichsen. **22–23:** Friends of Tualatin River National Wildlife Refuge. **24:** Upper Clackamas Whitewater Festival. **25–26:** Jeff Curtis, Portland Rose Festival Foundation. **28–29, 53–54:** Gwen Callahan. **29–30:** Kerry Finsand. **31:** Cider Summit Festivals/Alan Shapiro. **32–33:** Ken Panck. **33–34:** Deb Yannariello. **35:** Saké Fest PDX c/o Event Navigators, LLC. **36–37:** Organic Beer Fest. **37–38:** David Minick. **38–39:** Oregon Food Bank. **41:** City of Gresham. **42–43:** Slavic Heritage Festival. **43–44:** Oregon Brewers Festival. **45:** Hood to Coast Race Series. **46–47:** Portland Saturday Market. **47–48:** Dorcas Herr. **49:** Jeanne Levy. **52:** Vernonia Salmon Festival. **55, 112-113:** Oregon Cheese Guild. **56-57, 150-151:** Oregon Brewing Company. **58:** Literary Arts. **59–60:** Audubon Society of Portland. **60–61:** Holiday Ale Festival. **65:** Leslie Scott, Oregon Truffle Festival. **67:** Hoopla Association. **68:** KLCC. **69–70:** Mt. Angel Chamber of Commerce. **70–71:** St. James School: Shirley Gray. **72–73:** Oregon Ag Fest/Michele Ruby. **73–74:** Community Festivals Association. **75–76:** Willamette Heritage Center. **78:** Mount Pisgah Arboretum. **79–80:** Lebanon Strawberry Festival Association, Inc/Chelly R. Bouferrache. **81:** The Oregon Garden. **82–83:** Eugene Mission. **84:** Travel Salem. **85:** McKenzie Community Track and Field. **86–87:** Wildwood Musicfest. **88:** Salem Art Association. **89–90:** Homer Davenport Community Festival by Gus Frederick. **91–92:** City of Woodburn. **93:** Stephen Saxon. **94–95:** David Shewey. **96–97:** City of Carlton. **97–98:** Dave Jackson. **99:** Mount Angel Oktoberfest–Monica Bochsler. **101–102:** Peter Aslen. **103:** Dewey Weddington. **104–105:** Mt. Angel Hazelnut Fest. **109–110:** Oregon Shakespeare Festival–Eddie Wallace. **111:** Neuman Hotel Group/Karolina Lavagnino. **114:** Ashland Parks & Recreation. **115:** Britt Music & Arts Festival. **116:** Oregon Honey Products LLC DBA Nectar Creek. **117–118:** Sutherlin Blackberry Festival. **119–120:** Ashland Parks & Recreation Commission (APRC), Susan T. Sullivan. **121:** David Gibb Photography. **122–123:** Ashland Chamber of Commerce. **127, 158:** Angela Cardas/Cardas Photography. **128–129:** Fort George Brewery. **129–130:** Greater Newport Chamber of Commerce. **131–132:** Gary Hayes. **132–133:** City of Seaside Visitors Bureau. **133–134:** Merrianne Hoffman for Pacific City Birding and Blues Festival. **135:** Astoria-Warrenton Area Chamber of Commerce. **136–137:** Oregon Coast Council for the Arts. **138:** Linda Sherych. **139–140:** Florence Area Chamber of Commerce. **141:** Visit Tillamook Coast. **142:** Allie Towers Rice/ used under a Creative Commons Attribution-ShareAlike 2.0 Generic License,www.creativecommons.org/licenses/ by/2.0/. **143:** City of Lakeside. **144–145:** Astoria Scandinavian Midsummer Festival. **146:** Community Coalition of Empire. **158, 161-162:** Lincoln City Visitor & Convention Bureau. **149:** Southern Oregon Kite Festival Committee. **153, 160:** Coos Bay Downtown Association. **154:** The Mill Casino Hotel & RV Park. **155–156:** Gold Beach Brew & Art Fest. **157:** Astoria Downtown Historic District Association. **162:** Explorer Media Group. **167:** Breweries in the Gorge (BIG). **169–170:** Oregon Winterfest. **171:** Klamath Basin Audubon Society. **172-173, 204-205:** BearBoot Productions.

174–175, 221: John Shewey. 175–176: The Dalles Area Chamber of Commerce. 177–178: Oregon Department of Fish & Wildlife. 179: Dawn Talbott Ontario Area Chamber. 180: Aaron Switzer. 181: East Cascades Audubon Society. 183: Linda Stephenson. 184–185: Stacy Totiand. 186: Eric Peterson. 187: Wallowa Resources. 188–189: Wheeler County Bluegrass Festival, Alex Doll. 189–190: Baker County Unlimited. 191-192: Theodore Hampton. 193: Sue DeHaas. 194–195: Brian Vegter. 196: La Grande Main Street Downtown, Laura Lynch. 197: Jason Waicunas, Outdoor Viewfinder. 199: Deschutes River Amphitheater. 200–201: Painted Hills Festival. 202: Wallowa Valley Music Alliance, Ashleigh Flynn. 203–204: Sisters Folk Festival, Inc. 206–207: Chuck Anderson for Alpenfest. 208: Three Creeks Brewing Co. 209–210: Vickie Liskey for Merrill Lions Club. 210–211: Eastern Oregon Film Festival. 212–213: Klamath Snowflake Festival, Michael McCullough. 221: US Forest Service; Jeff Gunn.

JOHN SHEWEY is an itinerant Oregon-based photojournalist specializing in natural history and outdoors recreation. His work has appeared in dozens of magazines and he has authored numerous books, including *Oregon Beaches, A Traveler's Companion* (2017), *Birds of the Pacific Northwest* (2017) and *Classic Steelhead Flies* (2015).